Living with Children & Horses:

By Nancy Faulconer

NOTE: This guide is NOT intended as teaching material. It is simply intended to provide a perspective on children and horsemanship based on my own experience.

Table of Contents

Safety and Environment…………………………………	Page 7
Choosing Your Friends………………………………….	Page 17
Time………………………………………………………….	Page 25
Motivation – Focus on the Positives……………………..	Page 32
Motor Skill Development and Ages of Children…	Page 39
Choosing the Right Horse……………………………..	Page 43
Supervision…………………………………………………	Page 45
Going Forward - Practice Sessions…………………..	Page 49
Troubleshooting……………………………………………	Page 57
Building Respect – Defining Your Personal Space..	Page 63
Developing Willingness and Cooperation…………	Page 71
Developing a Winning Partnership……………………..	Page 79
Developing Safety and Control………………………………	Page 83

Children's Workbooks:
1. The Play Day
2. The Bath
3. Body Language
4. What Horses Can Give You
5. What Good is Grooming?
6. I Am The Leader
7. Body Language Defined
8. The Riding Lesson
9. Are You Ready to Ride?

NOTE: This guide is NOT intended as teaching material. It is simply intended to provide a perspective on children and horsemanship based on my own experience.

June, 2006

A Harrowing Experience Turned Good

I would like to share something that happened to me, so that it won't happen to you. A friend, with plenty of experience in transporting and loading horses, and I were attempting to load and deliver a horse that I had been boarding for another friend. After several hours and a sweaty, nervous horse, we got him loaded in the trailer. Until... the unthinkable happened. I was at the trailer door, waiting for my friend to come out, so I could shut the door, and we could be on our way. The horse was loose in the trailer, and it was getting dark, so he did not know that the door was almost shut. He barreled out the back, slamming the door into my face, knocking me to the ground, and to make matters worse, stomping all over me. Imagine 1,100 pounds of muscle stepping all over you. My poor fiancé saw the whole thing happen and my friend got to see me get stomped. After a long night in the emergency room, and seven stitches in my lip, (did I mention a missing front tooth?) I decided I would let someone else deal with this horse. He did not like trailers, and I was in no condition to attempt this again.

I was at the grocery store when I ran into Claire from Cloud9 Ranch. I told her what happened, and she did not hesitate to offer her help and assistance using Natural Horsemanship skills. She came over the next day, and got the horse to a comfortable level with the trailer. She wanted to come back again the following day, with her sister, Nancy Faulconer, who I have known and respected for close to seven years now. I got a call from Nancy saying that they had him relaxing and would be ready to trailer him to his new home later that afternoon. I am happy to say that Buddy is in his new home and rode in the trailer like a champ.

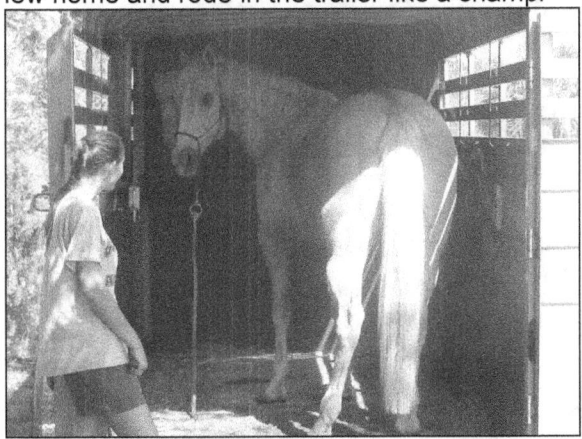

I was amazed how he "hopped" right in after a few short sessions. Some people don't believe in Natural Horsemanship, but I look in the mirror and I am the one with the split lip and missing tooth. SAFETY is the key here. Many many thanks to Nancy and Claire and Cloud9 Ranch for sharing what they know with others and helping prevent accidents like mine. If I had been a small child, I could easily have been killed! I have learned to re-think things for the future so this never happens to me again! I am lucky to be alive.

– Cathy Billger, Naples, FL

NOTE: This guide is NOT intended as teaching material. It is simply intended to provide a perspective on children and horsemanship based on my own experience.

I would like to dedicate this guide to my husband, who even though he is not a horseman, was patient and supportive during the process. I would also like to thank all the people who touched my life during this important period. Connie Smith of SW Florida Equine Rescue who profoundly impacted my horsemanship, and my instructor and friend Kirsten Nelsen (www.wexfordfarm.com) who consistently provided the right information when I needed it.

It is my hope that all who read this book will gain something from it and have a little more fun with their kids and their horses.

Living with Children and Horses

NOTE: This guide is NOT intended as teaching material. It is simply intended to provide a perspective on children and horsemanship based on my own experience.

Introduction:

This guide is NOT intended as teaching material. It is simply intended to provide a perspective on children and natural horsemanship based on my own experiences.

As a parent, it is YOUR responsibility to keep your children safe.

This includes proper footwear, attire and education. The most basic rule of safety is to make your children AWARE of personal space. A good way to explain this is to children is to stand them inside a hula hoop. The hoop represents their personal space and gives them a physical boundary (rather than an imaginary bubble).

The horse (any horse) should not be allowed to invade their space. Unconsciously, many of us move backward when a horse crowds us. To a horse, this indicates submission!

The horse becomes higher in status when he moves your feet.

Teaching kids this basic rule will prevent a lot of other problems from ever even occurring. As always, seek professional help if you are unsure of how to proceed.

Playing like this, with no halter or lead, is not for beginners! We have made sure that Sassy has respect for Jordan's personal space, and that Jordan knows how to position herself for control even without the halter and rope. It's not for beginners, but it is fun, and worth the effort to develop your skills to this point!

NOTE: This guide is NOT intended as teaching material. It is simply intended to provide a perspective on children and horsemanship based on my own experience.

Safety and Environment

This guide is written directly from my personal experience in developing my horsemanship using natural methods, studying psychology and communication of equines, and incorporating the aspect of having young children underfoot while learning. There are a few good natural horsemanship programs available, and the internet has many more resources. Please visit www.cloud9ranch.info if you need some direction on where to look for a good horsemanship program.

As you progress along your horsemanship journey, you will realize there are many parallels between parenting and horsemanship. I am presenting this guide as an attempt to invite you to think along the lines of what worked for my family, and hopefully spark your imagination and creativity where your own family is involved.

Some important considerations are safety and environment. If you expect your child to wear a helmet during their horse interactions, then YOU should be wearing a helmet. That decision is up to the parent, and must be enforced by the parent. My children have repeatedly shown me that my example is more powerful than my speech, and so I believe that modeling the behavior that you want them to learn is a top priority.

In all probability, it's not what you put ON your head that keeps you safe, it's what you put IN your head, and ultimately, in your children's heads. Knowledge and preparation will keep you safe.

In summary, safety and environment are going to play a major role in the success of your child's horsemanship.

NOTE: This guide is NOT intended as teaching material. It is simply intended to provide a perspective on children and horsemanship based on my own experience.

Things to Think About:

Horses have their own set of priorities! Things that are important to horses are:

- **Safety** (Horses are PREY animals... they are unsure of PREDATORS, which is what PEOPLE are!)

- **Comfort** (Horses gain comfort from defined leadership roles. They don't WANT to have to be the leader. They will be very happy if you are the leader, but you have to earn this position.)

- **Play** (Horses move each other's feet to establish dominance, they do this in every day interaction, and they make a game of it. It is wise for the parent to understand this, and to be very aware of what the horse is telling us.)

- **Food** (Again, leadership at feeding time is critical.)

Following are some of the most important points that I have had to address:

A relaxed, comfortable horse is a safe horse. By becoming a good leader for your horses, you will create willing and cooperative animals.

Using prey animal psychology is an excellent way to accomplish this. With children helping tend the horses, everything takes on MORE significance. Therefore, at feeding time, it is very important that you build RESPECT into this routine.

NOTE: This guide is NOT intended as teaching material. It is simply intended to provide a perspective on children and horsemanship based on my own experience.

My children like to help me feed the horses, so the method that I found to be safe and effective is lining the horse up to be fed.

What this means is that you approach the gate, stall door, or fence where the feeder is kept, and <u>you protect your personal space</u>. Do not allow the horse to push into you, or your children, in an effort to get to his breakfast faster. Using a broom or training stick like a windshield wiper is very effective. Most horses will only run into it once before they get the idea and wait patiently <u>out</u> of your 4 foot "bubble".

What is most important is that your horse **waits** until you have put the feed in his bucket, and his ears are up, before you allow him to come and have it.

If he tries to drive you by putting his ears back or snaking his head down, just keep blocking him with the stick until he backs up and gives you a nice look.

If your horse is particularly difficult, DON'T ENTER his space!

Stay on the outside of the stall or on the other side of the fence. If he absolutely refuses to wait, go back in the house!

Try again in a few minutes…. or an hour later. The difference this makes is amazing. All of a sudden, all of the other things I wanted to do with my horses became easier when I started defining leadership roles at feeding time.

NOTE: This guide is NOT intended as teaching material. It is simply intended to provide a perspective on children and horsemanship based on my own experience.

Here Jordan and Sassy play with follow the leader around the arena. Even the flapping tarp is not a distraction. They are a good team.

Regarding play, watch how horses interact with each other! One is a leader, and one is a follower.

The leader decides what game they are going to play, at what level, and for how long.

One of my favorite things to watch horses do is work out the pecking order of the herd. The one who moves his feet is demoted to lesser status, and the one who did the bossing is elevated. There are no equals in a horse herd.

There are NO EQUALS in a horse herd. That is important to remember when you are handling horses. I try to provide interesting objects for developing my horses trust and respect in my leadership.

When you are a good leader, you will find that introducing strange and exciting objects like generic pool toys (blow up octopi, noodles, balls, etc.) make excellent toys for use with your horse! My yearling likes to bite them, so I can't turn him loose with them or they don't last long.

Tarps are excellent for simulating crossing water, hanging on fences and from trees, and some kites have been good toys when the kids are finished with them. Also, beach canopies and umbrellas are good for going under. The main point is, use your imagination! These props can all be used for developing your horses tolerance to new things, and provide mental stimulation for him. By introducing new toys you will keep your skill development fun for your horse and pique his curiosity as well.

Sassy is not worried about the noisy tarp.

Living with Children and Horses

NOTE: This guide is NOT intended as teaching material. It is simply intended to provide a perspective on children and horsemanship based on my own experience.

Parent to Parent NOTE:

As a parent of two young children, I found the following strategies helpful.

1. **Talk About the Skills You Will Need**: When I was still struggling with my own skills, I would make up word games to play with the kids in the car.... We learned that horses move other horses to establish dominance. We learned that they use warning signals before they escalate their behavior to using their teeth and hoofs to move each other's feet. They make ugly faces, lay back their ears, stomp their feet, all in an attempt to warn the other horse that he should MOVE!

2. **Practice Without the Horse:** By role playing and taking turns being the horse and the human, my pre-school age kids could learn some basic concepts that would be helpful when they interacted with real horses. And they could not even read yet! We colored pictures of the parts of a horse. When I would practice with my training stick and string, they would too. We haltered the kitchen chairs. We turned lights off and on with our sticks... I found a shorter one for the kids, and it really helped that it matched their smaller size. We made up a card game with the ways that you can ask a horse to yield, and played it until they had them memorized.

3. **Get Some Experience**: When I was more confident in my own ability, I would put the bareback pad on my mare and let one child sit on the horse while I held the rope and practiced yielding and moving my horse around at slow speeds. Both kids developed terrific natural balance using this technique, and I never had to worry about run-away mounts **because** I still had the rope! We practiced the dismounting from a stop and a walk, and correct mounting procedures, and my little mare's patience grew and grew! The best thing I think was how comfortable she got wearing the saddle or bareback pad and looked forward to having the kids on board. It was a nice change from the high pressure performance world that she left behind! I went out of my way to make each session short and positive for both kids and equines.

NOTE: This guide is NOT intended as teaching material. It is simply intended to provide a perspective on children and horsemanship based on my own experience.

Tyler gets a lead line lesson.

An inflatable whale can even hitch a ride when your horse is not afraid of it!

Living with Children and Horses

NOTE: This guide is NOT intended as teaching material. It is simply intended to provide a perspective on children and horsemanship based on my own experience.

I discovered that it was much easier to build on small successes than to try to get a specific thing accomplished and maybe end up opening a can of worms that would take much longer than the time I had to spend on it.

Once I realized this, I became very patient. Mostly because being patient was the fastest way to realize results. All I had to do was set it up to be easy for the horse, and wait.

Regarding the learning environment, one of the most important points I would like to make is about a safety net, or play pen.... I used a 60 foot round corral at first, and graduated to a 80' x 100' arena. This is the safe area, with no trees, roof edges, bicycles, cars, mailboxes or other implements to get tangled up in. I almost want to say it goes without saying, but I have been to lots of other people's horse keeping areas, and they have everything BUT a safe area to play and ride and practice in. The side of the road is NOT a good clear area to experiment with if you are an adult with your horse, and it is definitely not going to be an asset to your success with a small child and horse combination!

You absolutely must have a safe, comfortable area where you can drop the rope if you need to, and not worry about where the horse will be when you pick it up again.

Riding while being led is an invaluable tool for developing balance and confidence.

Living with Children and Horses

NOTE: This guide is NOT intended as teaching material. It is simply intended to provide a perspective on children and horsemanship based on my own experience.

Choosing Your Friends

Getting comfortable with motorized vehicles

It is important to realize that, like it or not, everyone's actions are influenced by the people they associate with.

When I began my horsemanship journey, I had a small group of "normal" friends. We would trail ride together, do some local shows, and hang out. They also had kids the ages of my kids. Well, as you might have experienced, when you are developing your skills using natural horsemanship you have a significant lack of "grace". It's UGLY! It's clumsy, and it still works!

BUT my friends began calling me "Kum By Yah" and other silly names. My training stick with the bag on it terrified their horses, and I was increasingly uncomfortable with the example that they were setting for my young and impressionable kids! It's difficult, as an adult, to override the habits that you have from earlier horse experiences, and I suddenly realized that my kids did not have to go there!

Parent to Parent: This is a key area to look at in your own life. The "atmosphere" where your learning and modeling for your children will make or break the outcome. It is very important that you cultivate an atmosphere of supportive, like minded people. The attitude of competition, having to get the job done, or worrying about how other people think your horsemanship looks will end up defeating your efforts before you get started.

Jordan and Sassy getting ready for Halloween!

For my family, we decided to keep to ourselves until we had the new skills and tasks well within our comfort zone. We improvised an arena at home and stayed there. I politely became unavailable when my traditional friends wanted to go trail riding and they didn't even really notice that I was avoiding horsey situations with them. We still ate lunch, we still went to the movies on the weekends... we just didn't ride together! I took my horses to the trail, but we played with our horses by the trailer and had lunch. We didn't actually ride for about 6 months! My kids grew calmer and braver and we were all much safer.

Jordan and Dusty work on focus and balance without the pressure of an audience. (Just the camera)

The PARTY SCARE!

The most vivid memory in my mind of this time is from a birthday party for my daughter's 6 year old friend. Her mom had just bought her older brother a new horse, and they had them all tacked up and tied down and were doing pony rides during the party. As you can imagine, this was not the best idea! The mare was also young, in a new place, and did not even have the chance to get to know her people or her environment and now there was a party situation... I had learned by now what people think when you try to tell your friends about your natural horsemanship approach, so I kept my mouth shut. But I kept my eyes open, and my kids by my side. After about the third ride, the little mare was quite worked up, so up climbs the birthday girl, and away she goes! She rocketed all around the property, jumping pedestrians with cake, dodging balloons, and ejecting her passenger. Luckily, no one was hurt. They then put the horse away (imagine what she was thinking) and decided that it was not a good idea to have her out in the party.

Parent to Parent: The point is, my kids knew better, I knew better, and we did not participate in that disaster, BUT we also did not try to take over and make the other people adopt our viewpoint. We discussed it later, at home, and I stressed to the kids that you can not MAKE someone understand what we are trying to accomplish through natural horsemanship, but that the best idea is to become a model of good behavior and hope that catches their attention.

My friends probably don't remember these little "moments" like I do, but they were really important to me as I made decisions concerning my horselife.

There will be sacrifices that you will make, you may miss an entire show season!

Living with Children and Horses

NOTE: This guide is NOT intended as teaching material. It is simply intended to provide a perspective on children and horsemanship based on my own experience.

You may not trail ride for six months or more, but trust me, when you do return to your "discipline" or favorite equine activity, it will be a whole lot more rewarding and enjoyable.

On the other hand, as we played the Natural Horsemanship exercises together, we started to develop our own version of "fun" things to do with our horses and made some new friends. One of my favorites is the annual Halloween Costume Contest. Everyone wins a prize, and it's great fun.

Jordan and Kylee with Buckshot

Mystical Teaspoon is a Unicorn for the day!

We have also had fun with ground skills tournaments, and give everyone a chance to try their skills. It's a fantastic learning opportunity too.

The most important thing to keep in your mind when planning to attend activities is: "Is it safe for my children?" If you are not sure if you can trust the other people involved, or you have any doubts to the type of environment, it is best to wait until your entire family has the skill level they need to be safe. A high, stress, competitive environment is unsettling to kids <u>and</u> horses.

Treasure stands on the tire. Can she put all 4 feet in?

Living with Children and Horses

NOTE: This guide is NOT intended as teaching material. It is simply intended to provide a perspective on children and horsemanship based on my own experience.

The Horse Show!

As my skills progressed, I decided to try a local show with my 6 year old daughter and her pony. I was the only parent who walked alongside, just in case. Another child was in tears, and her pony had dragged her out of line and would not stand still for the halter class. I should have known better!

While we were there, my kids witnessed a local man loading a terrified yearling into his trailer. He was cussing, whipping, and pulling for all he was worth. They still talk about it. It was so unnecessary!

During the Pee Wee Walk Trot Class, again, I walked alongside. The announcer came on and said there would be no points for my daughter if I had to touch her or her horse. Hmmm... is it worth the points if my daughter needs my help and I am in the bleachers? NO!

So, on we went. She did not need my help, but several of the others sure could have used a different type of support from their parents! The same little girl who was in tears at halter class, was again in tears as her parent/coach screamed at her to "KICK HIM! Don't let him stop at the gate!"

Jordan was more worried about that yelling parent than the other horses in the ring with her! I was very glad that I was walking right there. After the class, another parent said to me, "I think you may have the right idea."

When it comes to choosing your friends, there is quite a lot you can do. Choose your activities wisely, stay in the arena, round pen or other secure environment and focus on developing your skills and modeling appropriate behavior.

This also applies to boarding situations. If you have your horse at a barn where you are the only one doing natural horsemanship, then stay away from everyone else!

Find a quiet spot and work on yourself. If your children are with you, let them sit nearby and watch. Coloring books, card games, and other quiet activities give you the chance to focus and help keep them from becoming bored. I used to think my kids were not paying attention when they were playing, but then they would surprise me with how much they learned.

Parent to Parent: If other people put you down, or make unkind remarks during your skill development, the way that you handle this is also a model to your children.

I always get a kick out of playing dumb! When someone said something like, "That's ridiculous!" but made sure I could hear them, I would respond very politely, "Thank you! You too!" and continue about my business. They either think I misunderstood, or they think I am crazy, either of which is fine with me. I am not doing this for anyone else, so their opinion is irrelevant. The bottom line is you need a supportive mental attitude, and you need to separate yourself from anything that will interfere with you reaching your goal.

My dream is to become such a good role model that my kids will be great role models! Then we can go out into the world secure in our abilities and enjoy our horses safely.

NOTE: This guide is NOT intended as teaching material. It is simply intended to provide a perspective on children and horsemanship based on my own experience.

TIME

Playing off line is more challenging, and more fun!

This is perhaps the most challenging of the variables to control... Time! There never seems to be enough of it. I have come up with some creative ways to incorporate "horsey" time into our driving time, bedtimes, and rainy day times. The idea of role playing is a natural way for kids to experiment with the ropes and training stick and string, and to practice their feel. In the case of my two kids, one would be the horse and one would be the human... it's an excellent way to find out just how soft you can be with the string!

Parent to Parent: Don't turn two kids loose together at first! They need to understand how to use the tools in a manner that will not result in injury to one or the other. Again, preparation is the key.

We took turns, and I would be the human and one of my children would put their hands out in front of their body and "wear" the halter.

Living with Children and Horses

NOTE: This guide is NOT intended as teaching material. It is simply intended to provide a perspective on children and horsemanship based on my own experience.

We played yielding the forehand and hindquarters and moving out of our personal space this way. Once they were adept at the motions, then I would allow them to be creative and experiment with one or the other of them being the horse! A challenging twist is to make it a rule that they can't use their voices. This may turn into a game of charades, but it is a good way to reinforce the importance of non-verbal communication.

We made a card game that the kids can take in the car, to help them remember what each game is about. I like to photocopy pictures of horses too, and use them for coloring, dot to dot, identifying the parts of the horse, etc.

Parent to Parent: It's up to you to keep the children safe and interested in the activity. I believe that it is important to evaluate the willingness of the children and the horse prior to each day's interaction.

At the end of the day, it is not so much what you have accomplished that matters, but that you have approached it with the attitude that every interaction is a building block.

The timeline may be longer than you originally intended, but if you take it a day at a time, and plan to stick to it, without any pressure of accomplishing a particular goal, then you can have confidence that it will work.

NOTE: This guide is NOT intended as teaching material. It is simply intended to provide a perspective on children and horsemanship based on my own experience.

Big Problems...

I have found that "trying" to do too much is a sure recipe for frustration! The other day, after a full day at kindergarten, my son came home off the bus already tired. He tried to groom and play with his horse, but he was really not in the right mental frame of mind to be at his best. Shortly afterward, he collapsed in tears. I took him right in and gave him comfort! Dinner, bath and bed. As much as it was a nice night, we all had the free time, and the horses were cooperative, it was just not the right time **for Tyler**. Going forward, I will make it a priority that energy level of the children is sufficient for them to expend the effort that horses require!

For my daughter, this meant that we only had hands on horse time on Saturday and Sunday. She was just not able to handle school, homework and horses on the same day of the week. In spite of this, we still managed to progress on her horsemanship by reading together at night, and role playing and talking about horsemanship, dominance and some of the psychology during our other activities together.

The self portrait is the favorite pose!

The idea of reverse psychology also applies to the children. Sometimes, I tell them to go play in the yard, visit the swing set or catch bugs, or even experiment with the digital camera (carefully) and release the pressure of even doing anything horsey off of the kids. Often, some of the most interesting perspectives can be shared through the camera lens☺

Jordan, Sassy and me, sharing a secret.

Most importantly, it's not the number of hours they spend, it's the attitude they bring to the time that they have. It should always be fun!

Driving a cart is fun!

Play "Put Your Nose on Dad"

My daughter tended to be less adventurous and even timid at times. I tried to be encouraging in order to boost her confidence, but the big breakthrough finally came when I acknowledged her fears, and told her, "I don't care if you EVER ride your pony again. If you like grooming and working with her on the ground, that's all that matters."

Once I said that, I could not keep her OFF the pony. Now, three years later, I can't keep her off any of the horses on the property.

Tyler does not ride as much as Jordan, but even so, when he does get the urge to ride it usually turns into a contest. Jordan will challenge him to do whatever she can do, and he does pretty well to keep up. This turns into lots of games on it's own.. Simon Says, Follow the Leader, etc.

For the younger kids, one day a week may be a lot! Remember, it's not the goal, it's the process. You are not only building relationships with the horses and kids, you are building habits of responsibility and respect. You may be surprised how much your relationship with your children will grow during the journey.

Living with Children and Horses

NOTE: This guide is NOT intended as teaching material. It is simply intended to provide a perspective on children and horsemanship based on my own experience.

Motivation - Focus on the Positives

Wise people know, anyone can MAKE their horse get in a trailer... but do you know how to make your horse WANT to get in?

Once you've got a new skill, try to do it in SYNC with someone else! That adds a whole new degree of challenge!

Parent to Parent: It's YOUR job to keep your kids safe, and interested in spending time with the horses. Try to keep it fun!

Putting It All Together

Living with Children and Horses

NOTE: This guide is NOT intended as teaching material. It is simply intended to provide a perspective on children and horsemanship based on my own experience.

Now imagine, you've done the preparation, you've cleared the schedule, you have arrived at the barn... and you want to make the most of your time. So, what do you do when either your horse or your child (or both!) don't seem to be as focused as you do?

This can be a HUGE source of frustration. Realize that frustration comes from setting goals (big goals) and pushing subconsciously toward them. Try to keep things simple. There is quite a lot that can be accomplished in the barn aisle. Think in terms of the pieces, the parts of the bigger things that can easily be tuned up on a low key day. If you can break it down to the simplest elements, you will find a thousand little successes to celebrate.

For example, you have gotten to the barn. Let's see how your session will go:

Does your horse greet you at the gate? YES! Great, ask him to face you and bend his head to be haltered. NO? Slow down, wait to be acknowledged. Maybe offer a rub or a pat and retreat. Grab a drink and come back in a minute. Take a seat and wait. See if he changes his mind about saying hello....

Does your child seem interested in helping? YES! Great, give her a task that you know she can do well and praise her for it. Acknowledge her contribution. When she successfully completes the thing you requested, then you may ask for another task. NO? Give her an alternative activity. Reading, drawing, bug collecting, listening to music quietly.

Depending on the age of the children, you can reach agreements that are mutually beneficial. My children love to be allowed to stay up later, so I let them stay up as long as they are using their pitchforks to clean stalls. One night they cleaned 6! (1 each is required, any extra is extra).

NOTE: This guide is NOT intended as teaching material. It is simply intended to provide a perspective on children and horsemanship based on my own experience.

Be flexible! If the grooming and ground skills exercises go well, add in an extra challenge or two... if you don't get that far every time, don't worry! There is no expiration date on horsemanship. And, of course, the greatest challenge in horsemanship is mastering ourselves... This can be especially challenging for little ones!

I know some of you reading this are thinking, "SURE! After I work all day, get home, and get to the horse, I am supposed to be happy with the littlest thing?" And the answer is, if you aren't, you'll find that for every time you push past the comfort zone of the horse or your little humans, it will take you the next two or three sessions to recover the ground that you lost when you pushed. Suddenly, standing there in the midst of chaos in a little bubble of tranquility becomes a lot easier.

My daughter continually pushes my buttons. She is so much like me that I have had to develop a lot of self control to avoid "going there". And, oddly enough, it's not as much fun for her to throw a fit and carry on when I am not responding to her. Communication can not occur when one or the other of you is emotional! So, if she's not talking to me in a normal tone of voice, I will not answer her. I simply take deep breaths and remind her of the "rules". When she regains her composure, then we can communicate again.

In a strange way, relating to the children in a fair manner has improved my leadership skills and natural horsemanship has improved my parenting by reminding me how important using phases and following through are.

The more consistent you are with this, the more they want to please you. Also be sure to set them up to feel successful. Don't give them jobs that they can't do well.

NOTE: This guide is NOT intended as teaching material. It is simply intended to provide a perspective on children and horsemanship based on my own experience.

Jordan and Kylee play "Follow the Leader"

My children are NOT perfect! But I also have good friends who will not sugar coat. They told me my daughter was disrespectful… hmmmm…. and once I was made aware of it, I took steps to build respect with her, using phases, and being consistent.

Thank you Natural Horsemanship!

PARENT TO PARENT: Instead of saying, "No, that's not right!" in correcting your child, I found that if I told them, "It's hard for me to tell you how to do it, let me show you once, and then you can see if you understand." Then, they felt less criticized and more capable.

After a few tries, I found that before I could interrupt in an attempt to "help" my children had worked it out and made the corrections on their own.

Jordan and Tess playing with carrying the flag.

Parent to Parent

Reality Check: There are going to be setbacks! There are going to be days when you would really really like to go and enjoy your horse BY YOURSELF.

Do it! I took advantage of babysitters and my non horsey friends often while the kids were really little, (under 5) and it really helped accelerate my progress. The quest for better horsemanship is about <u>self development</u>.

The horse already knows what he needs to know. Keep this in mind, and you will discover new perspective and new comfort in the way you view your interactions with horses <u>and</u> with people.

<u>Parent to Parent: There were a lot of frustrating days, especially before I developed competency handling the rope, before I could use it for "feel" and my balance and timing got better.</u>

Depending on your situation, boarding, work schedule, study time, etc., you may decide that it is best <u>not</u> to bring the kids and horses together at all before you have a reasonable amount of proficiency yourself.

I have a backyard stable and I board a few horses for other people, who are also natural horsemanship students, and we share the arena, round pen and common areas. Some of them also have children.

In this case, I could not just decide not to involve my kids.

They have learned everything they know from our example.

They were too young to read when we began our natural horsemanship program, and were disinclined to be "coached" by their mother in front of the other people!

So, I literally stopped everything I was doing each time one of my friends needed support, and tried to be an example of a good student. We would find the answers together, and everyone would learn from the experience. This modeling and positive atmosphere is a key element of our success.

Patience is easier to attain when you realize it is the fastest way to get the results you want!

Some days all I would accomplish would be monitoring the kids on the swing set so the other boarders could do the chores. But

---
NOTE: This guide is NOT intended as teaching material. It is simply intended to provide a perspective on children and horsemanship based on my own experience.

surprisingly enough, we found that we used steady and rhythmic pressure when we were asking the horses to move with us from stalls to turnout, and to stand quietly, without being tied in cross ties during grooming.

By paying attention to these seemingly insignificant parts of our horse life, the bigger things became much more within reach.

The end result is that my supportive group of friends and I are all making progress. Our environment is enhanced by our positive attitude, and even a day where nothing is really accomplished becomes a good day at the barn.

Another issue that will come up is "Am I pushing horses on my kids?" The answer will be YES. They are kids.

They are not going to be able to decide what they *REALLY* want to do until they are about 25. (At least that's how long it took me to get my act together!)

So, until then, **you** make the rules. There are lots of choices out there and many sports and activities available. When you sit down and think about it, all are costly, and involve transportation, regular practices, and an investment of your time and commitment.

Each program has advantages and things that they will teach your child. I considered this, and chose to use the horsemanship program to develop positive traits in my child, with me as the coach.

The horse/human relationship is a fantastic one for developing respect, consideration, emotional control and responsibility.

I also like that it's NON Competitive, and appropriate for our children's physical development. So many sports put more emphasis on the outcome, or winning, than what it takes to excel.

Again, more important than what you are actually doing is the attitude you bring to it. It should be fun!

NOTE: This guide is NOT intended as teaching material. It is simply intended to provide a perspective on children and horsemanship based on my own experience.

Motor Skill Development & Ages of Children

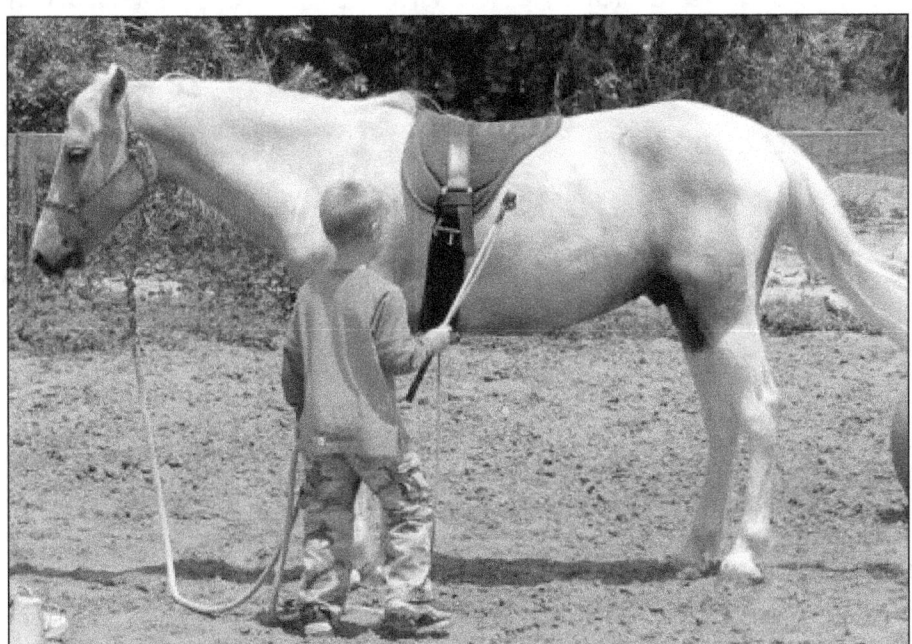

Tyler learning to use the rope and training stick

Consider the following data from Kinderstart:

Between ages two and three:

Gross Motor

runs forward well
jumps in place with two feet together
stands on one foot (with aid)
walks on tiptoe
kicks a ball forward

Fine Motor

strings four large beads
turns single pages
snips with scissors
holds crayon with thumb and fingers (not fist)
uses one hand consistently in most activities
imitates circular, vertical, horizontal strokes
paints with some wrist action; makes dots, lines, circular strokes
rolls, pounds, squeezes, and pulls clay

NOTE: This guide is NOT intended as teaching material. It is simply intended to provide a perspective on children and horsemanship based on my own experience.

Children under 3 should be closely supervised. They do not possess the physical coordination to be able to do much with horses. Their main focus is on their own bodies. With a 3 year old, I would recommend you always hold hands and keep a close watch on them.

Between ages three and four:

Gross Motor

- runs around obstacles
- walks on a line
- balances on one foot for five to ten seconds
- hops on one foot
- pushes, pulls, steers wheeled toys
- rides tricycle
- uses slide independently
- jumps over six inch high object and lands on both feet together
- throws ball overhead
- catches a bounce ball

Fine Motor

- builds tower of nine small blocks
- drives nails and pegs
- copies circle
- imitates cross
- manipulates clay material (rolls balls, snakes, cookies)

Children ages 3-4 should still be closely supervised. They are gaining control over their own motor skills, and can do much more than before, but supervision should be very close at hand and never forget that the size of these young children puts them right under the horse's nose, in the blind spot.

They need to be taught exercises to protect their personal space, and tactics to become more visible to a horse at close range. These exercises include, jumping jacks, raising and waving arms to back the horse up out of their space, and always holding the hand of their supervisor.

NOTE: This guide is NOT intended as teaching material. It is simply intended to provide a perspective on children and horsemanship based on my own experience.

Between ages four and five:

Gross Motor

    walks backward toe-heel
    jumps forward 10 times without falling
    walks up and down stair independently, alternating feet
    turns somersault

Fine Motor

    cuts on line continuously
    copies cross
    copies square
    prints a some capital letters

Children 4-5 should be closely supervised. They can probably assist with grooming, stand on the mounting block for extra height, and help with retrieving items when asked. Sessions with real horses should be kept short, but this age loves to color and play games about horses and horsemanship. Reading stories together is also valuable, and they will learn a lot from role playing.

Between ages five and six:

Gross Motor

    runs lightly on toes
    walks on balance beam
    can cover 2 meters hopping
    skips on alternate feet
    jumps rope
    skates

Fine Motor

    cuts out simple shapes
    copies triangle
    traces diamond
    copies first name
    prints numerals 1 to 5
    colors within lines
    has adult grasp of pencil
    had handedness well established
    pastes and glues appropriately

Children 5-6 should be supervised. Depending on the child, concepts presented are grasped quickly, but be sure to be consistent! Role playing and reading and writing stories are favorite activities for this age, and riding a quiet horse with a parent leading will develop balance and coordination needed for independent riding later.

NOTE: This guide is NOT intended as teaching material. It is simply intended to provide a perspective on children and horsemanship based on my own experience.

Motor skill development is important to keep in mind when asking your child to do certain things! My daughter was 6 before she could master the fine motor skill of closing one finger on the rein at a time. Following sequential directions is also tough for younger children.

Again, my supportive circle of friends intervened. "Be sure she can physically DO the thing you are asking her to do." That seems obvious, but the challenge is when you are immersed in it, you are sometimes too close to see the obvious things.

Again, this logic applies to young horses as well as young kids. It is a good idea to practice skills like running forward and backing up with another human as a role model horse prior to practicing the same skills with an actual horse on the line!

As a 36 year old adult, I had to practice running backward before I became good at it! Attitude is the key. Keep it fun and you will enjoy the awkwardness as you learn.

I was taking a lesson once when I was so clumsy and tripping and wrapping myself in the strings and ropes that I could not help but laugh!

"You must want to laugh at me!" I blurted. I'll never forget her reply as she shook her head and grinned at me, "Been there, done that!" I have found that being willing to make mistakes, and to experience my own learning curve with my friends and my children builds their confidence in making mistakes in front of me.

NOTE: This guide is NOT intended as teaching material. It is simply intended to provide a perspective on children and horsemanship based on my own experience.

Choosing the Right Horse or Pony

Is he a good match?

I had the "perfect" small horse all picked out for my daughter before she was even ready! Belle is a 14.2 hand spotted saddle mare that I had raised from birth. She was our "lesson pony" for years before we went natural, and she was very cooperative and safe for anyone to handle. But, my daughter never "took" to her. She viewed Belle as everyone's horse, and wanted one that would be all her own, and special only for her.

At first, I balked. "How unreasonable!" I thought. "She's a 5 year old child! She's lucky to have a horse at all!" But then, I tried to imagine the world through her eyes. She had no conception of the financial aspect involved in providing her with a horse, or the time or responsibility of owning an animal. So those arguments are invalid. We had paying boarders, we had room, so I asked her, "Why do you need your 'own' horse?" Her answer was a good one. "So I can put the bareback pad on all by myself."

I learned a good lesson that day. And, in a blinding flash of the obvious, I learned to listen to my own advice. I always tell people that it is important not only that you understand what to do, but that you can DO it yourself. Hmmmm….

In an instant, my forty pound daughter made an excellent case for herself. The search was on for a suitable pony. We looked at several over the next few weeks. Each one was rejected for different reasons, but each one provided us with valuable insight into what we were NOT looking for.

We got creative at finding ways to interview the prospective ponies, in spite of the best intentions of the presenting owners in trying to demonstrate to us what each fabulous pony could do.

I would bring a drink with me, and casually shake the ice to see if the pony had a good tolerance for strange noises. We would arrive to the appointments a bit early, to witness the owner "catching" the pony. I did not take my daughter along on these shopping trips, but I did bring along my digital camera for her opinion afterward. She wanted a perfect pony, but she also wanted a beautiful pony!

We tested how each little mount reacted to being saddled, bridled, and led around on a loose rein. We asked to see them being clippered, having their feet picked up, and backing up. We asked about their feeding routine and veterinary care.

Most importantly, we asked why they were being sold. During this process, my friends and I learned quite a few things to be aware of when buying a pony. We were also able to accomplish the task without alienating any of the people we talked with, and without riding the horse.

Supervision

Jordan practices asking Sassy to go over obstacles.

This chapter addresses allowing your child to explore their growing skills, at the appropriate level.

It assumes that the other points addressed in earlier chapters have been adhered to, that your child knows what the Natural Horsemanship exercises are, has the skills to apply them, and that they have appropriate motor development to handle the tools.

It assumes that you are in an appropriate arena or round pen, and have a suitable horse.

NOTE: This guide is NOT intended as teaching material. It is simply intended to provide a perspective on children and horsemanship based on my own experience.

With all these things given, I have found that my children are very good at applying the concepts to a variety of situations. My daughter has a lot of fun pushing a large ball around our arena, with her pony on line.

She is also very good at standing all 4 feet on the tire or platform.

She likes the on line activities and at this point, I give her a lot of freedom to explore. I believe she is reasonably safe because she has the skills she needs to be able to keep the pony out of her personal space.

The little freedoms I give her she has earned. She can now approach her pony and halter her unassisted. She is developing good grooming skills and knows how to teach her pony to stand in the aisle without being tied. I insist on spotting her (standing close by, with the lead in my hand) when she cleans the feet. Since she has demonstrated solid safety skills on the ground, she is allowed to mount and dismount unaided, and ride in the yard and arenas.

Jordan asks Buckshot put his front feet in the trailer.

NOTE: This guide is NOT intended as teaching material. It is simply intended to provide a perspective on children and horsemanship based on my own experience.

My son is just 5 and he is allowed few of these freedoms.

His rules are that someone (myself or one of the other natural horsemanship students) is beside him, offering guidance or taking the rope.

He basically does riding and moving with the pony while we move the pony's feet and direct his pony. He can, however, tie the bareback pad and halter knots correctly on his own. He also likes to show off!

Now, at age 8, he rides very well. He just does not do it as often as his sister. He still needs more supervision and has less confidence. I have noticed that he is a lot more interested when it is a contest than just recreational riding!

Tyler plays Hulk with Teaspoon.

NOTE: This guide is NOT intended as teaching material. It is simply intended to provide a perspective on children and horsemanship based on my own experience.

Tyler and Dusty communicate on line.

<u>**Parent to Parent: The most important thing to remember about supervision is that by example, you are instilling in your child the most important things that he or she need to know.**</u>

<u>**By setting a good example and being a positive role model, when the time comes for the child to make his or her own decisions you will not have to worry, because they will know what to do. They won't even have to think about it.**</u>

For me, watching this develop was one of the most special things. I hope this helps you get a sense of what is possible.

Going Forward - Practice Sessions

Time flies when you are having fun!

It has now been three years since I started introducing horse psychology and communication concepts to my kids. We are now riding well, and have progressed beyond the confines of the round pen and small arenas.

We are going out into the world, and attending horse events. This chapter addresses practice sessions, and how to keep them positive for both horse and children.

The main concept to remember in preparation for anything is positive reinforcement. It should be fun! Try not to worry that there is a show in X number of days, and all that stress that comes with it.

Keeping in mind that the whole reason we are into horse stuff anyway is for relaxation and recreation, make your goals realistic, and attainable. Don't jump in the deep end over your head!

This past weekend, we attended a local barrel race. It was a prize winning, money paying event, and there was some big competition there.

I kept my kids grounded and enjoying it, by reminding them that we are not competitive barrel racers. We were there to enjoy the day and have our horses enjoy it too.

The times were in the 16 and 17 second range. My kid's times were 24 and 25 seconds, but we had a good time, we enjoyed the day and each other.

Remember, you can not control what the other parents and kids are doing. There were some scary moments when little kids strapped to big, high powered horses rocketed around the arena on the barrel pattern with the child sobbing.

That is certainly one way to introduce your child to riding and competition, but I am glad it was not the path I chose.

Each time we practiced, we did not drill any particular event, we worked on a feeling of lightness and togetherness with our horses, and we tried to keep it interesting. Going out of the practice pen, taking the riding to the pasture and even down to the mailbox and back can help prevent turning your hobby into a chore.

Games to Develop More Independence

The Game is - Keep the Pony Between Your Legs and Hands

Developing a young riders awareness of how his or her body can affect the way the pony goes is an advanced, important skill. I have found that the best way to get them to understand it is to make it a game.

Here, Tyler is looking to the left, and opening his left hand and arm, and also his left leg, but Dusty is looking to the right. After a step or two, Tyler helped out a little more with the rein on getting Dusty to understand where Tyler was wanting to go.

I think this is preferable to just dragging the horse around by the reins. It also promotes thinking on the part of the child and the horse.

Simon Says, "Put All Four Feet in the Water."

For "Simon Says" the riders get to give each other things to try to do - like putting all four feet in the water, and then backing out. Of course, I am on hand to make sure things go well, and I have had the horses in the pond before, and I am sure it is safe to go in before I allow the kids to try this.

Back your horse over a pole, while you are sitting in a chair.

Use your imagination for fun with friends. Here, I am asking Treasure to go backward, over the pole.

For horse soccer, I got a blow up soccer ball and the kids take turns pushing it with the horse's nose or feet into the goal.

This game is best played at a walk!

Another fun game is a variation of soccer with a plastic bag on the end of a training stick. Again, before we play this one we are sure the horses are familiar with the plastic bag on the stick, and unafraid of it waving around them.

The Game is - Horse soccer with an oversized ball and a flag on a stick.

Mom does the preparation, before the kids are turned loose to play the game.

We've done this one so many times now that Jordan is quite handy at getting new horses ready to play. She understands when to quit, and I am very happy with her self confidence. I am still sure to be available to supervise and assist as needed.

I hope this short guide has giving you some things to incorporate into your own horse lives.

Please feel free to email me at www.cloud9ranch.info with comments and questions.

NOTE: This guide is NOT intended as teaching material. It is simply intended to provide a perspective on children and horsemanship based on my own experience.

Troubleshooting - When Things Go Wrong

Horses are not motorcycles. They don't stop and turn off and remain parked when we are finished riding them. They think and react for themselves. If you are a parent who has had horses personally, you know the risks. That is my main goal in writing this book, to help raise awareness in the mind's of the parents.

Developing a partnership means earning the horse's trust. If a dog explodes out of the woods (even if it is YOUR dog) and the horse does not feel safe in his environment, he will spook.

That is not something you can train out of him.

It is something you can prepare for, and practice for, and always be mindful of.

So, what happens when things go wrong?

My daughter ate the dirt in a big way one morning when our dogs bounded out from the bushes behind her pony.

Luckily, no one was hurt, and it opened our eyes to the fact that we needed to set up more practice sessions with fast moving objects approaching from behind with that pony.

By not over-reacting, and by understanding that the nature of the dogs and the nature of the horse is all that happened, there is no blame placed, no punishment required. It would be counter-productive to get upset in this situation.

Slowing things down, and going back to an area where safety, confidence and balance can be redeveloped is important.

In order to prevent things from going wrong, it is important to start out slowly, practicing basics until the horse and rider have developed a communication system with working brakes, steering and relaxation.
Staying within the confines of a fenced riding area and having safety procedures in place like helmets, and knowing how to quickly dismount and land standing on your feet are good ideas to implement.

Practicing carrying flags, walking on tarps and past moving, flapping banners is all part of a smart PROACTIVE troubleshooting strategy.

If you have an accident, it is important to take the time it takes for the return of confidence.

It is also important to develop practice exercises to strengthen skills like balance, coordination and leadership in order to prevent a re-occurance.

With friends, it is a good idea to challenge the riders to line up, three in a row, and then walk together, go around a corner together, and back up together.

This will help them fine tune their riding skills without making the exercise a tedious drill. It is fun! But be sure that it is excellent at the walk, before you have them try it at a faster gait.

For developing balance, I like to have the kids ride in a bareback pad without stirrups.

They ask the pony to walk, and they push on the withers, and feel how the horse's movement affects their bodies.

We experiment with faster walking, and then trotting and cantering. I have a line on the pony. The riders have no reins.

In this way, we develop the ability to balance with the horse at each different gait.

If the horse goes faster than the rider intended, they do not have the option of snatching at his face to get him to slow down. Instead, they get the opportunity to slow down in their own body, and experiment with how that can translate to their horse to relax and slow down.

As a backup, I have the line and the horse is only going around in a circle anyway, so he can not run off with the rider.

After this is excellent on line, I allow the kids to have reins, but not use them unless it is necessary.

These are good basic exercises that are outlined in depth in many natural horsemanship training programs.

I see the benefits of a good foundation and I highly recommend that developing an excellent set of basics be a priority for every horse involved family.

Building Respect – Defining Your Personal Space

As a parent, it is YOUR responsibility to keep your children safe. This includes proper footwear, attire and education.

The most basic rule of safety is to make your children AWARE of personal space. A good way to explain this is to children is to stand them inside a hula hoop. The hoop represents their personal space and gives them a physical boundary (rather than an imaginary bubble).

The horse (any horse) should not be allowed to invade their space. Unconsciously, many of us move backward when a horse crowds us. To a horse, this indicates submission! The horse becomes higher in status when he moves <u>your</u> feet.

Teaching kids this basic rule will prevent a lot of other problems from ever even occurring. As always, seek professional help if you are unsure of how to proceed. It is better to invest some time and money having a professional help you troubleshoot, than to give it a shot on your own and end up with a hospital bill or a develop a bad habit in your horse that could have been prevented!

In summary, safety and environment are going to play a major role in the success of your child's horsemanship.

NOTE: This guide is NOT intended as teaching material. It is simply intended to provide a perspective on children and horsemanship based on my own experience.

Things to Think About:

Horses have their own set of priorities! Things that are important to horses are:

- Safety (Horses are PREY animals… they are unsure of PREDATORS, which is what PEOPLE are!)

- Comfort (Horses gain comfort from defined leadership roles. They don't WANT to have to be the leader. They will be very happy if you are the leader, but you have to earn this position.)

- Play (Horses move each other's feet to establish dominance, they do this in every day interaction, and they make a game of it. It is wise for the parent to understand this, and to be <u>very</u> aware of what the horse is telling us.)

- Food (Again, leadership at feeding time is critical.)

Bubba meets us for the picture, but does not push his way into our space.

Living with Children and Horses

NOTE: This guide is NOT intended as teaching material. It is simply intended to provide a perspective on children and horsemanship based on my own experience.

Following are some of the most important points that I have had to address:

A relaxed, comfortable horse is a safe horse. By becoming a good leader for your horses, you will create willing and cooperative animals. Using prey animal psychology is an excellent way to accomplish this. With children helping tend the horses, everything takes on MORE significance. Therefore, at feeding time, it is very important that you build RESPECT into this routine.

My children like to help me feed the horses, so the method that I found to be safe and effective is lining the horse up to be fed.

What this means is that you approach the gate, stall door, or fence where the feeder is kept, and <u>you protect your personal space</u>. Do not allow the horse to push into you, or your children, in an effort to get to his breakfast faster. Using a broom or training stick like a windshield wiper is very effective. Most horses will only run into it once before they get the idea and wait patiently <u>out</u> of your 4 foot "bubble".

What is most important is that your horse waits until you have put the feed in his bucket, and his ears are up, before you allow him to come and have it. If he tries to drive you by putting his ears back or snaking his head down, just keep blocking him with the stick until he backs up and gives you a nice look.

If your horse is particularly difficult, DON'T ENTER his space! Stay on the outside of the stall or on the other side of the fence. If he absolutely refuses to wait, go back in the house! Try again a few minutes or an hour later. The difference this makes is amazing. All of a sudden, all of the other things I wanted to do with my horses became easier when I started defining leadership roles at feeding time.

To develop respect for your personal space and cooperation with a horse, it is important to realize that pressure is what motivates a

---

NOTE: This guide is NOT intended as teaching material. It is simply intended to provide a perspective on children and horsemanship based on my own experience.

horse to perform. If you bring on pressure too quickly, you will get a reaction. Not a response.

As soon as the horse makes an attempt to do the right thing, release the pressure! Stop jumping, and relax. Now, start counting. Don't move on to the next thing until you have had a chance to count to 60!

You will be amazed at how this simple addition of dwell time will improve your horse's attitude and wanting to try.

Building in yields on the ground, transfer to the riding in helping your horse understand how to yield to leg and rein pressure, not lean against it.

When you have demonstrated to your horse that you are a good leader, even in the resting times, her ears and attention will be on you.

In the spirit of developing willingness and cooperation, remember, good horsemanship is based on communication. Not a dictatorship. In order for communication to occur, the horse and the human must be sharing the same idea. It should not be the human, forcing his ideas on the horse.

For a prey animal like the horse, voting to give leadership to a human is a great act of trust and respect. When you have earned your horse's trust and respect, you are creating a very good foundation for mutual willingness and cooperation.

When your horse looks at you this way, you know you have a true partner. More resources are available.

There are a lot of great books on natural horsemanship and resistance free training. Remember, every minute you spend with your horse, you ARE teaching him. It is your responsibility to learn as much as you can, and to keep learning.

Developing Willingness & Cooperation – Preparing Your Horse for the Farrier

Getting a horse ready to have his feet worked on is a series of small steps. All the steps ultimately come together to help the horse understand what is expected of him when the farrier arrives.

To develop willingness and cooperation in a horse, it is important to realize that pressure is what motivates a horse to perform. If you bring on pressure too quickly, you will get a reaction. Not a response. The same is true for developing willingness and cooperation in a child.

Try to present the task in a manner that is fun and engaging for both horse and human. As soon as the horse makes an attempt to do the right thing, release the pressure! Stop everything, and relax. Now, start counting. Don't move on to the next thing until you have had a chance to count to 60! You will be amazed at how this simple addition of dwell time will improve your horse's attitude and wanting to try.

Preparation Step 1:
Can you ask your horse to stand quietly? Look at the two photos above. In the first photo, Treasure is cooperating, but mentally she is not relaxed. You can tell because her head is up and tense. A few seconds later, she relaxes and drops her head below her withers. It is important that you learn to recognize this, and don't ask for her feet before she is relaxed.

After your horse can stand quietly when asked, see if you can rub her legs all over with the rope. Gradually increase pressure until you an have her give you her foot when you apply pressure to the rope.

Preparation Step 2:
Stretch the leg forward like the farrier will do when the foot is put up on the stand for rasping.

Living with Children and Horses

A key to preparation is SIMULATION. Do what you can to mimic what will be asked of your horse. Keep the sessions short, and try to make it fun.

This is easy for some horses, and others take lots of small sessions spread over a few days or a week.

Living with Children and Horses

NOTE: *This guide is NOT intended as teaching material. It is simply intended to provide a perspective on children and horsemanship based on my own experience.*

Preparation Step 3:
Teach your horse to hold her leg up for you. Don't pick it up for her. Squeeze the chestnut and wait for her to pick up her leg. As soon as she tries, release! Now let her think about it for a minute.

Preparation Step 4:
Repeat this process every day for a week. You will be happy with the result. Allowing your horse to give you her feet is much more considerate than tying her up and taking her feet when you want them. If you will make this exercise a program for a week, you should see a big difference in your horse's attitude toward having her feet handled.

Preparation Step 5:
Don't assume that once your horse accepts having her front feet handled, she will be okay about her back feet. You should check her reaction to having the rope touch her back end and rear legs before you do it with your hands.

Preparation Step 6:
Once your horse can stand quietly while the rope wraps her back legs, you can ask her to give her back foot to you.

Again, ask for the foot. Pinch the skin at the cap of the hock, and wait for her to pick it up for you.

Ask and release when she makes an effort. This may take a few repetitions, but it is well worth the time invested. Don't forget the dwell time! Let her think about what you asked. It's okay if this process takes 5 days for the front feet, and 5 days more for the back feet. It is still much faster and easier in the long run than dealing with a scattered unprepared horse at farrier time!

If you are not present when your horse sees the farrier, be sure that you ask him how the horse behaves. Or if possible, change your appointment so that you can be there. It's your responsibility that your horse knows how to have his feet handled and is not worried about the trimming or shoeing process.

NOTE: *This guide is NOT intended as teaching material. It is simply intended to provide a perspective on children and horsemanship based on my own experience.*

In the spirit of developing willingness and cooperation, remember, good horsemanship is based on communication. Not a dictatorship. In order for communication to occur, the horse and the human must be sharing the same idea. It should not be the human, forcing his ideas on the horse.

For a prey animal like the horse, giving his feet to a human is a great act of trust and respect. When his foot is restrained, he can not use his greatest survival tool, the flight response. So, in allowing your horse to give you his feet, you are creating a very good foundation for mutual willingness and cooperation.

Developing a Winning Partnership – Preparing Your Horse for COMPETITION!

Competition is a big step! There are a lot of things to consider when you decide you want to go to a horse show. The horse that is your sweet willing trail riding partner may not be equipped to make the transformation to fancy show pony without a little work on your part.

Going to a show can be very rewarding. Here are some things to consider first:

1. **Go to the show WITHOUT your horse**. Take this opportunity to ask questions, observe other horses and riders. Watch for how the horse is presented, and what the riders are wearing. Decide which classes would be best for you and your horse. Fill out membership forms and pick up applications in advance so you can be prepared when your show day arrives. If you are unsure of the rules for showing or judging, now would be a good time to ask the person in charge for more information. There is nothing more frustrating than NOT KNOWING why your horse did not win that ribbon!

2. **Brush up on your trailer loading skills**. Remember, the easiest way to mess up your chances for being competitive are to have a trailer loading challenge on show day! Plan ahead, and practice loading your horse at least once a day for the seven days before the competition. I like to finish each practice session in the arena with a trailer loading and then I reward my horse for loading in the trailer by letting her rest in there for 10 minutes or so. The trailer can become a comfort zone for your horse.

3. **Evaluate.** Based on the information that you got when you went to the show, look at your horse and yourself objectively. Are you presentable? Are you dressed as well as the other competitors? Does your horse look his best? Is he groomed properly and in his best physical condition? Your chances of

---

NOTE: This guide is NOT intended as teaching material. It is simply intended to provide a perspective on children and horsemanship based on my own experience.

success are greatly reduced without attention to each of these areas.

4. **Practice the basics:** If you are going to a speed competition, you may be tempted to practice everything at full speed. But, if you think about it, and study the people who have truly mastered your event, you will find that mastery of the basic maneuvers **at a walk** is the key to a winning time. Remember the old rule of thumb: If you can't walk it perfectly, you shouldn't be trotting. If you can't trot it perfectly, DON'T LOPE! If you are preparing for a western or English performance

---
NOTE: This guide is NOT intended as teaching material. It is simply intended to provide a perspective on children and horsemanship based on my own experience.

class, you will still be smart to break down each task into it's basic components and get these really good.

5. **Dress Rehearsal:** If you can arrange it, setting up a mock competition at a location other than your usual practice area is a good way to gauge your strengths and areas for improvement. If possible, trailer your horse to a practice area that his is unfamiliar with, and have a pretend judge to give you feedback. If it is possible, have someone VIDEO you so you can watch it back later, and critique yourself.

Now, you've done the preparation and show day is just around the corner! Think positive thoughts and have fun! After all, that's why we have horses, isn't it?

Developing Safety and Control

Safety and Control begin on the ground. It is important that you are able to direct your horse's feet while you are on the ground, BEFORE you ever consider riding him.

Catching and Haltering:

It is important that your horse WANTS to be with you. You should not have to chase him down to catch him. He should be glad to see you approach. He should stand quietly, and bend his head toward you while he is being haltered.

Living with Children and Horses

NOTE: *This guide is NOT intended as teaching material. It is simply intended to provide a perspective on children and horsemanship based on my own experience.*

Leading

When you are leading your horse, he should match your speed and walk WITH you, not pulling ahead and not dragging behind.

Pre-riding Checklist:

Can you:

Gently push your horse's neck and shoulders away from you?

Living with Children and Horses

NOTE: This guide is NOT intended as teaching material. It is simply intended to provide a perspective on children and horsemanship based on my own experience.

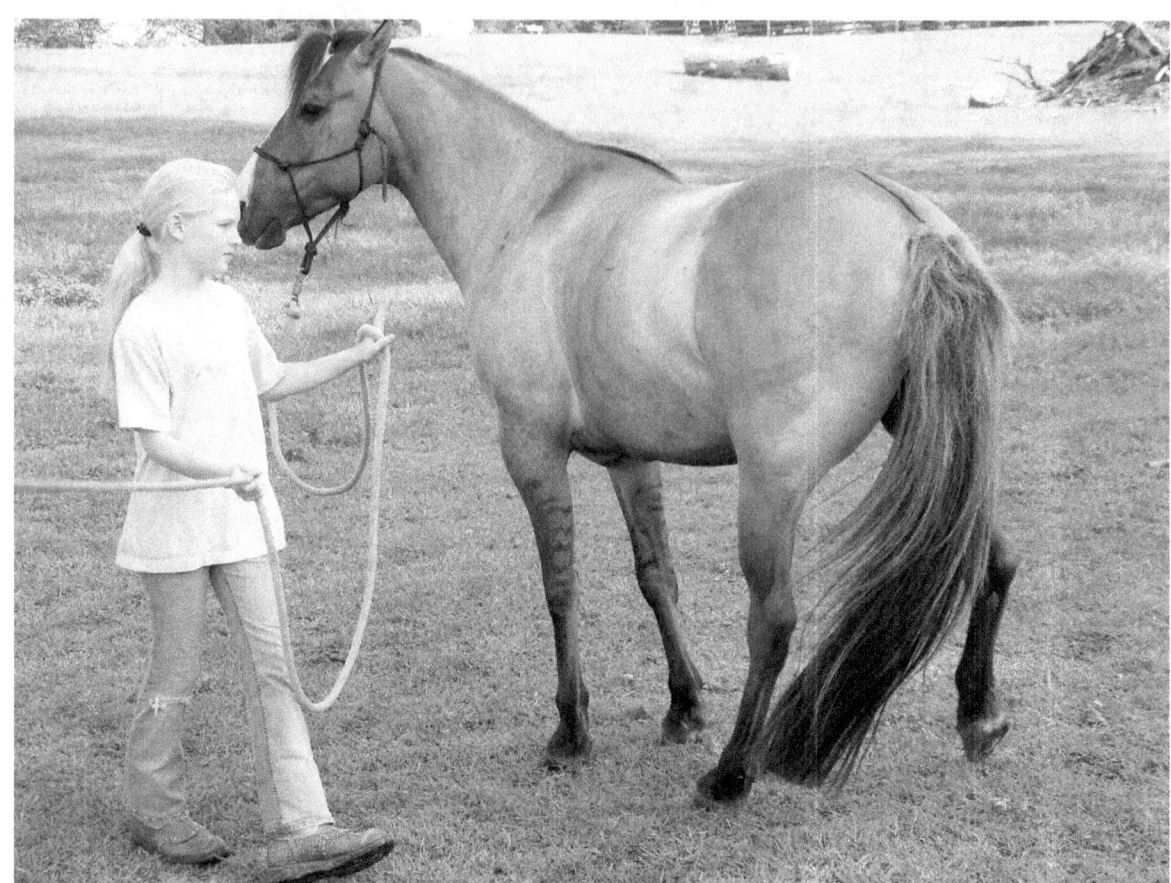

Pre-riding Checklist:

Can you:

Walk into your horse's space, and have him yield his hips away from you?

Don't forget the other side!

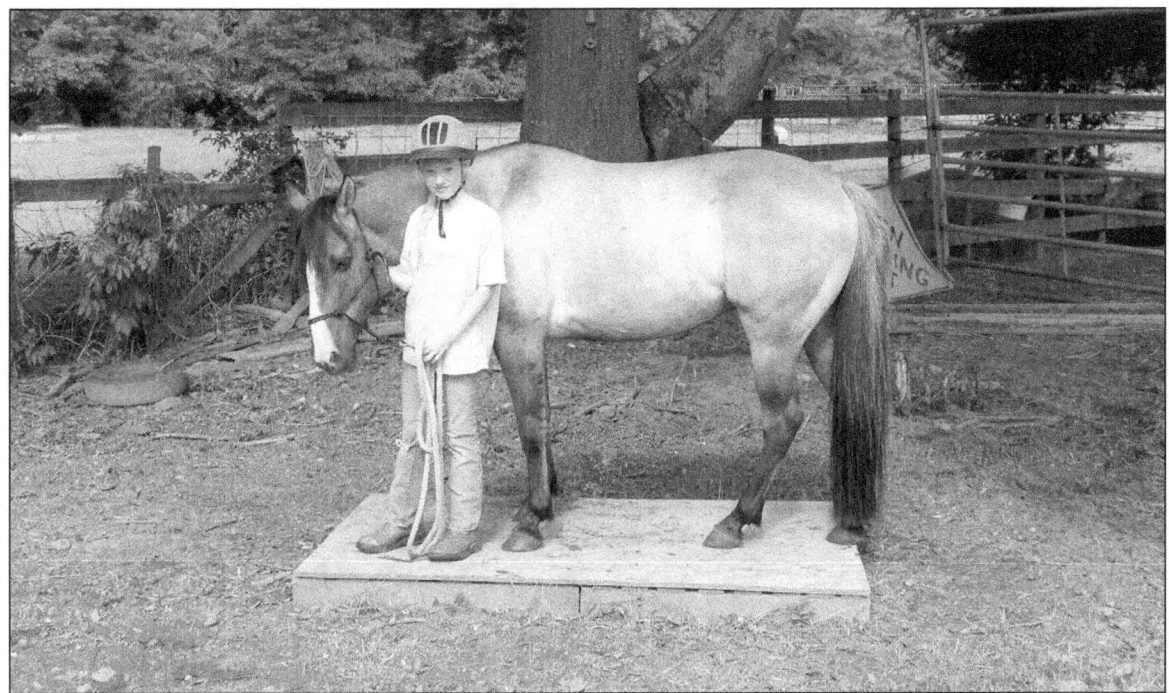

Pre-riding Checklist:

Can you:

Approach a platform or log or tarp and have your horse confidently go with you? And stay there?

Living with Children and Horses

NOTE: This guide is NOT intended as teaching material. It is simply intended to provide a perspective on children and horsemanship based on my own experience.

Pre-riding Checklist:

Can you:

Stand even with his ribcage, (where the saddle goes) and still direct his feet as well as you want to when you are riding?

Living with Children and Horses

Pre-riding Checklist:

Can you:

Approach a scary object and investigate it?

Pre-riding Checklist:

Can you:

Ask your horse to go over or past the scary object and have him remain relaxed and curious?

Once these pre-riding items are great, you will be surprised how good your riding can get!

Pre-riding Checklist:

Can you:

Ask your horse to come stand beside a block and wait for you to get on?

If your horse says, "No" you may want to do more exercises on the ground before riding.

Living with Children and Horses

NOTE: *This guide is NOT intended as teaching material. It is simply intended to provide a perspective on children and horsemanship based on my own experience.*

Pre-riding Checklist:
Can you:

Have someone else hold the rope while you ride without stirrups or reins?

Living with Children and Horses

Get it good at the walk before you trot!

Pre-riding Checklist:

Can you:

Relax and enjoy this! This is VERY IMPORTANT to develop your seat. And your horse will say "Thank you!" for not leaning on his mouth for your balance.

There is no limit to what your imagination can develop for you and your horse!

Remember, have someone help you, until you are confident and independent enough to explore a little on your own.

The Play Day

Today we had a play day!
Some of our friends came over, and we all played with our horses together.

Living with Children and Horses

NOTE: This guide is NOT intended as teaching material. It is simply intended to provide a perspective on children and horsemanship based on my own experience.

Tyler asked Dusty to jump over the log.

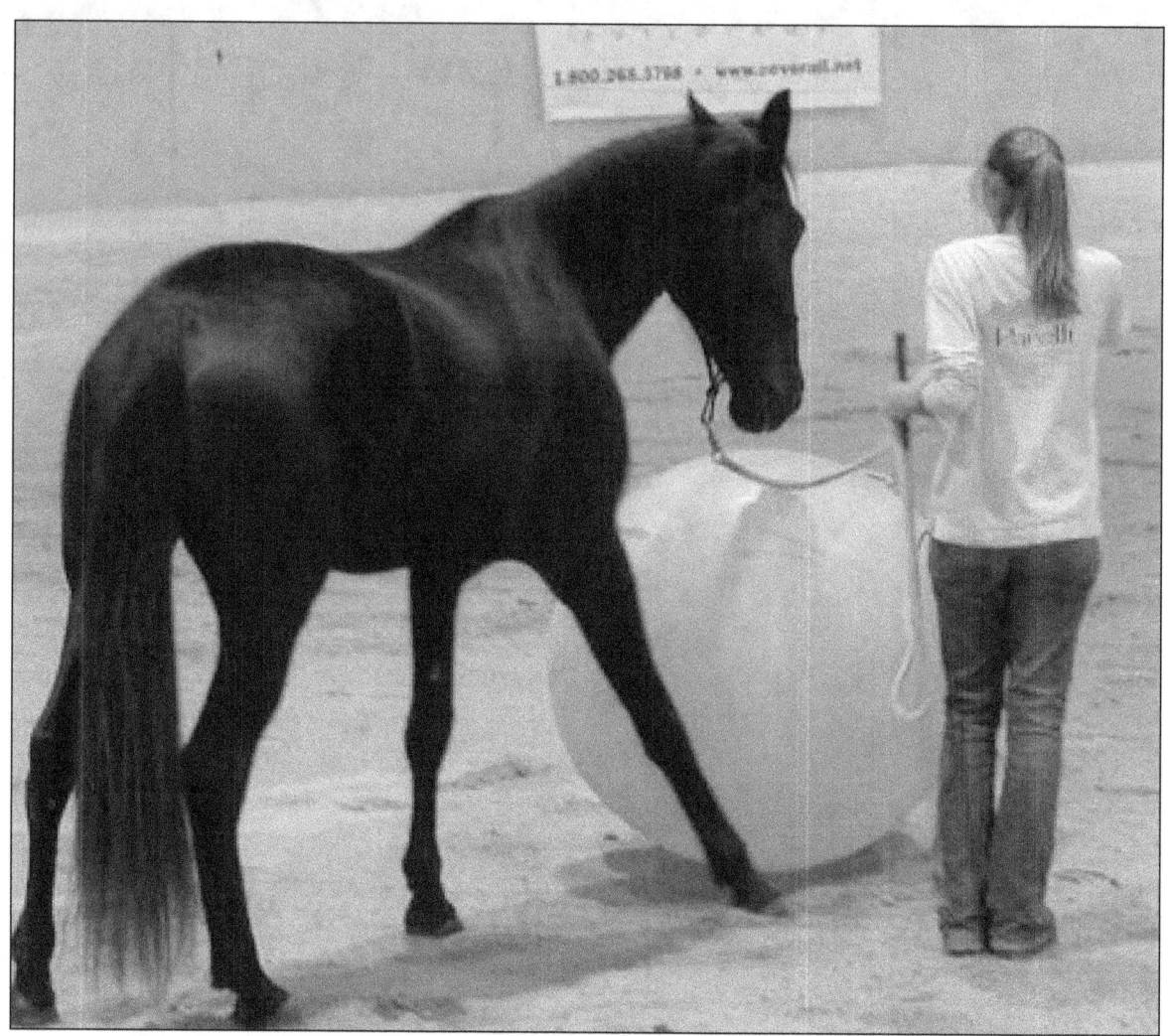

Claire and Majestic pushed around the big green ball.

Bandit got dressed up, he wore his green and purple noodle.

We played "PUT YOUR NOSE ON" the barrel, "Simon Says" and other games.

I think we all had a good time!

Living with Children and Horses

NOTE: This guide is NOT intended as teaching material. It is simply intended to provide a perspective on children and horsemanship based on my own experience.

The Bath

Living with Children and Horses - 99 -

NOTE: This guide is NOT intended as teaching material. It is simply intended to provide a perspective on children and horsemanship based on my own experience.

Parents Note: These pictures show how things SHOULD look! Lots of loose ropes, relaxed body language and confident horses who are used to being handled in every area of their bodies. You should not ASSUME that your horses will react the same way. Seek help from a qualified professional if you have issues that are beyond your current skill level. As your awareness rises, your competency will grow. Please visit www.cloud9ranch.info for more references. There are a lot of great books on natural horsemanship and resistance free training.

Remember, every minute you spend with your horse, you ARE teaching him.

It is your responsibility to learn as much as you can, and to keep learning.

Thank you, and Happy Horsing Around!

www.cloud9ranch.info

NOTE: This guide is NOT intended as teaching material. It is simply intended to provide a perspective on children and horsemanship based on my own experience.

Bathing Day

First, get your tools ready. A hose with a spray nozzle is easiest.

*The most important thing to remember is: both you and the pony should ENJOY the bathing process.

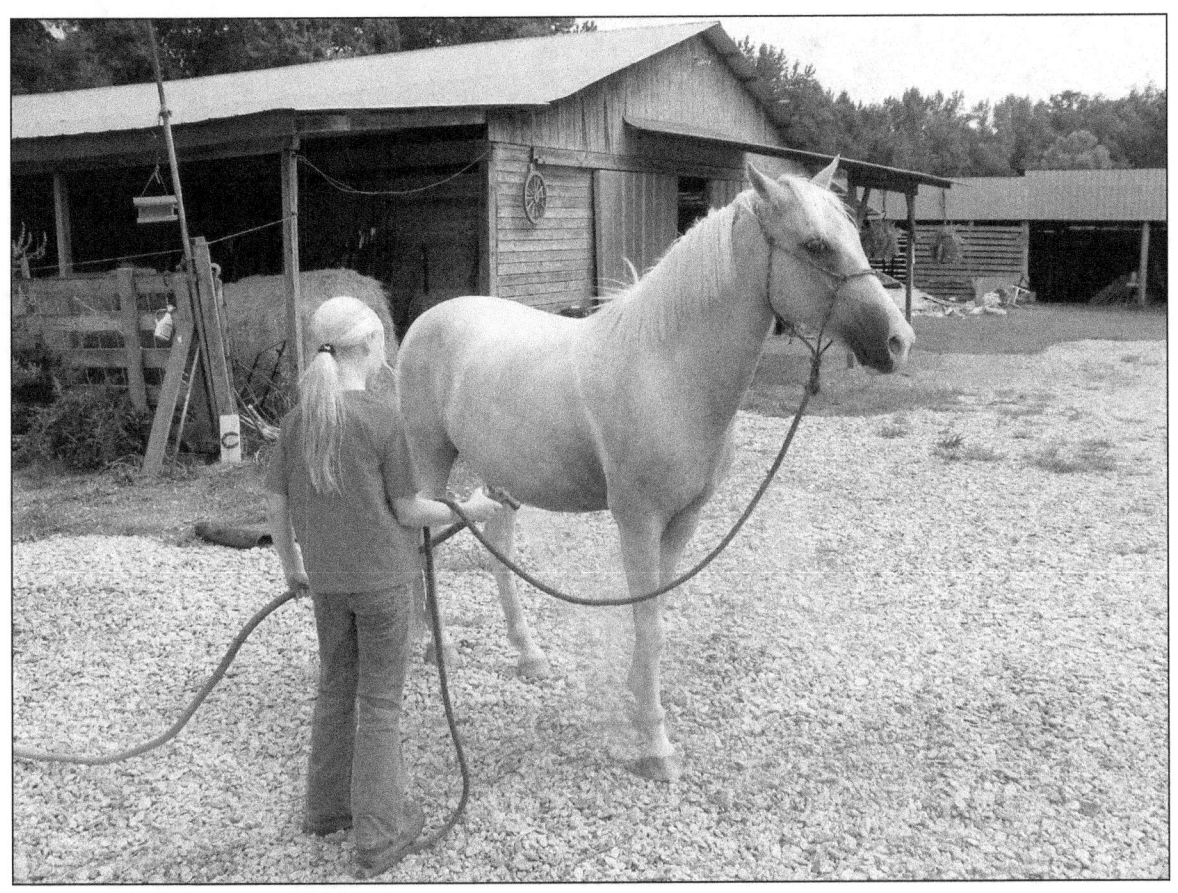

Choose a clear area, where you can tie your horse safely.

Here, Dusty is not afraid, so we ground tie him for this bath. He can move his feet if he wants to. Since he does not feel trapped, he is going to get curious about the bath.

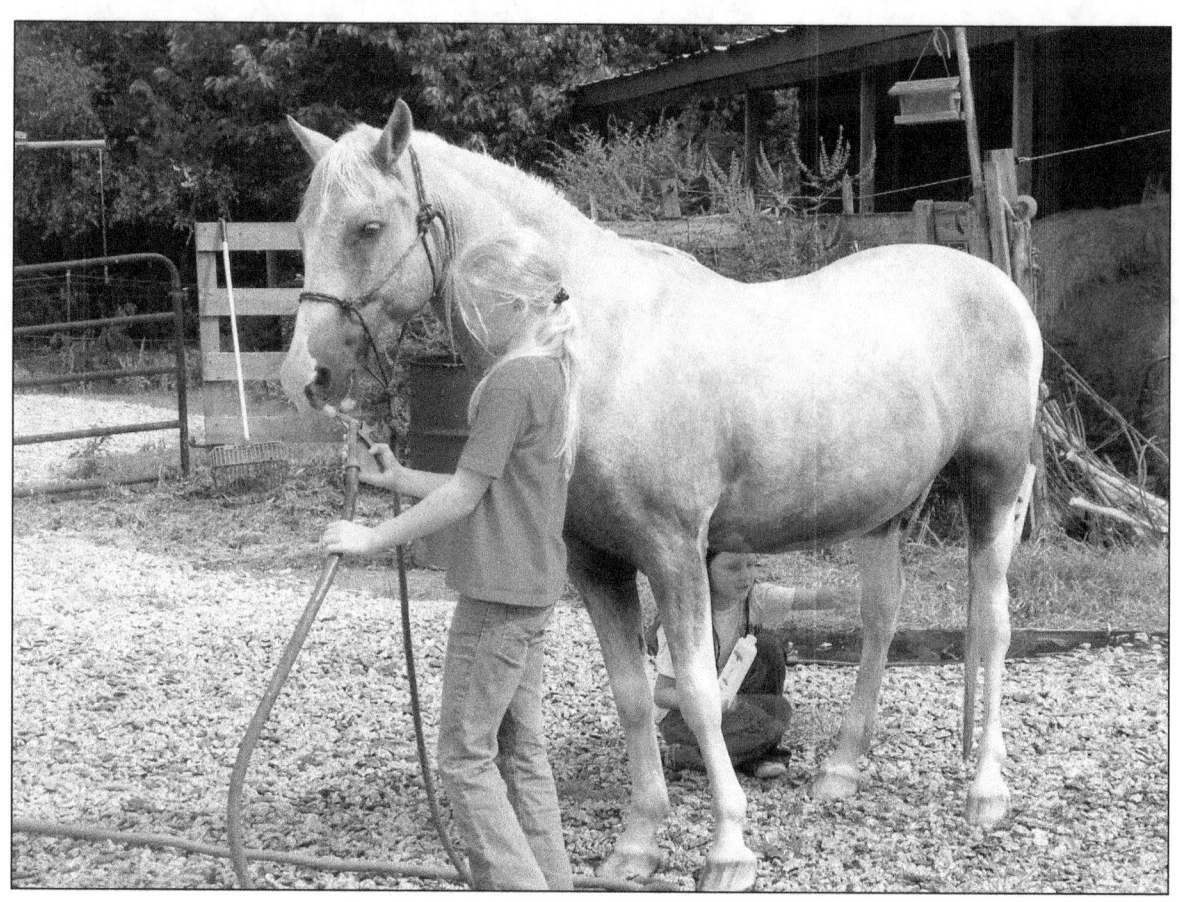

Begin by showing the pony the hose.
Let him smell it.
Then, gently spray his feet and front legs.
Stand to the side in case he wants to move his feet.
He may move a little, but if you are patient, he will stand still.

Living with Children and Horses

NOTE: This guide is NOT intended as teaching material. It is simply intended to provide a perspective on children and horsemanship based on my own experience.

First wet one side, then
wet the other side.
When the horse is wet,
then you can add shampoo.
Don't spray the pony harshly.
Spray him like YOU would want
to be sprayed.

Living with Children and Horses

NOTE: This guide is NOT intended as teaching material. It is simply intended to provide a perspective on children and horsemanship based on my own experience.

To wash the pony's face, start with asking him to drop his head.

If he just drops it a little, release the pressure and let him know that's what you wanted.
Repeat this until he can drop his head, when you wash his neck up to his ears.

Living with Children and Horses

NOTE: This guide is NOT intended as teaching material. It is simply intended to provide a perspective on children and horsemanship based on my own experience.

If he acts like he's worried about having you wash his cheek, go back to his chest, or front legs.
Retreat to an area he's comfortable with.
If you don't push him too far, he will grow more confident.

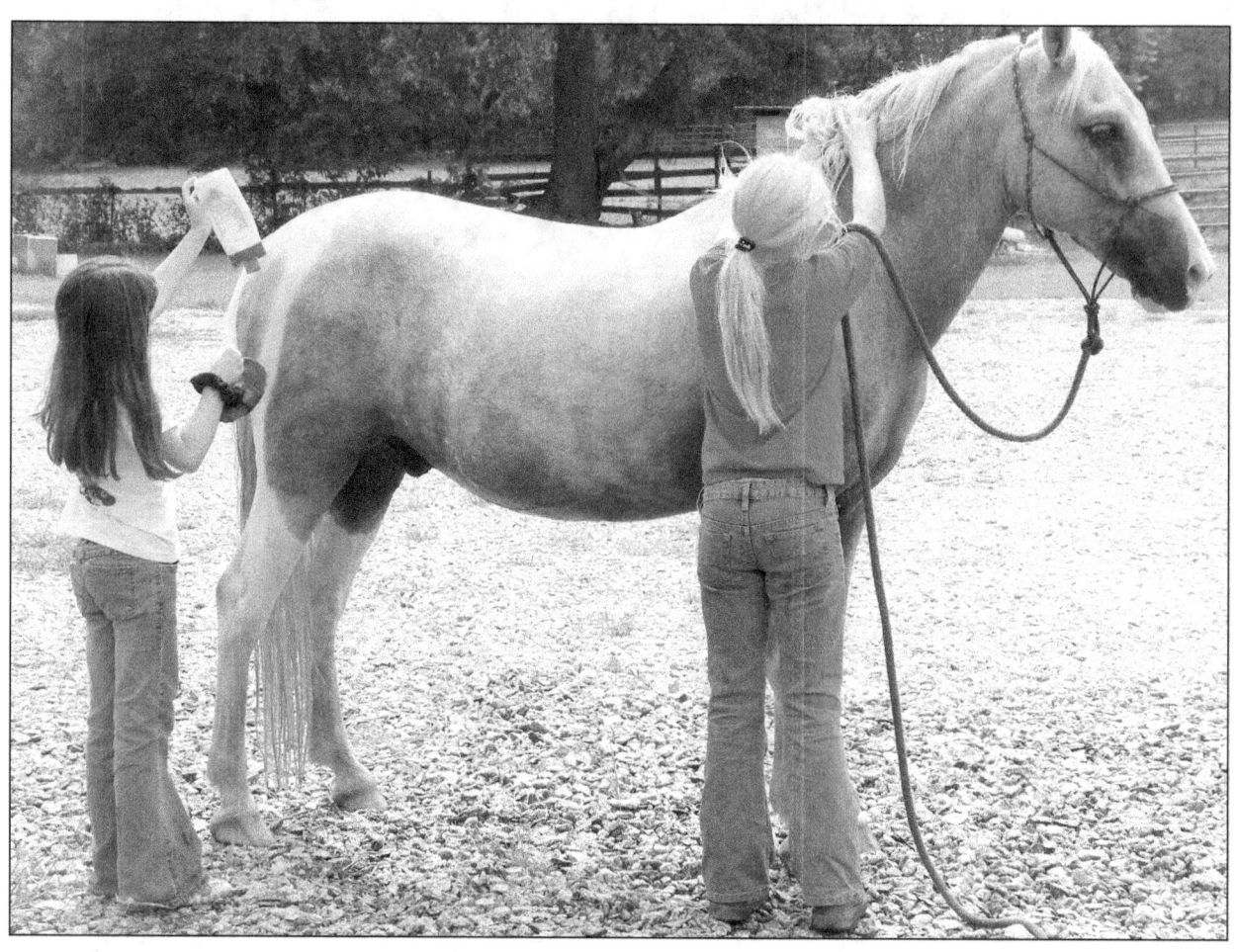

After you put the soap on, take your time and rub it in well.

If your pony starts to yawn, it's a good sign that he's relaxed!

Living with Children and Horses

It is important to wash all the way down to the feet.
Take care to rinse all the soap off your pony.
If you leave any soap, it can cause his skin to itch.

Don't be in a hurry! Giving a good horse bath takes a while.

It took a half-hour for us to wash this pony today.

Living with Children and Horses

NOTE: This guide is NOT intended as teaching material. It is simply intended to provide a perspective on children and horsemanship based on my own experience.

Giving a bath is a valuable way to build your relationship.

A pony will trust and respect you more if you can give him a good bath without scaring him or being rough.

Living with Children and Horses

When the rinse is complete, be sure you remove the extra water with a sweat scraper. That way, the pony will feel dryer, and is less likely to roll.

You can hang out with your pony and let him graze, or take him for a walk until he is dry. Giving our pony a bath is fun for us, and for the pony!

Body Language –

What Your Horse is Telling You

NOTE: This guide is NOT intended as teaching material. It is simply intended to provide a perspective on children and horsemanship based on my own experience.

Parents Note: These pictures show how things SHOULD look! Lots of loose ropes, relaxed body language and confident horses who are used to being handled in every area of their bodies. You should not ASSUME that your horses will react the same way. Seek help from a qualified professional if you have issues that are beyond your current skill level. As your awareness rises, your competency will grow. Please visit www.cloud9ranch.info for more references. There are a lot of great books on natural horsemanship and resistance free training.

Remember, every minute you spend with your horse, you ARE teaching him.

It is your responsibility to learn as much as you can, and to keep learning.

Thank you, and Happy Horsing Around!

www.cloud9ranch.info

Body Language – What Your Horse is Telling You

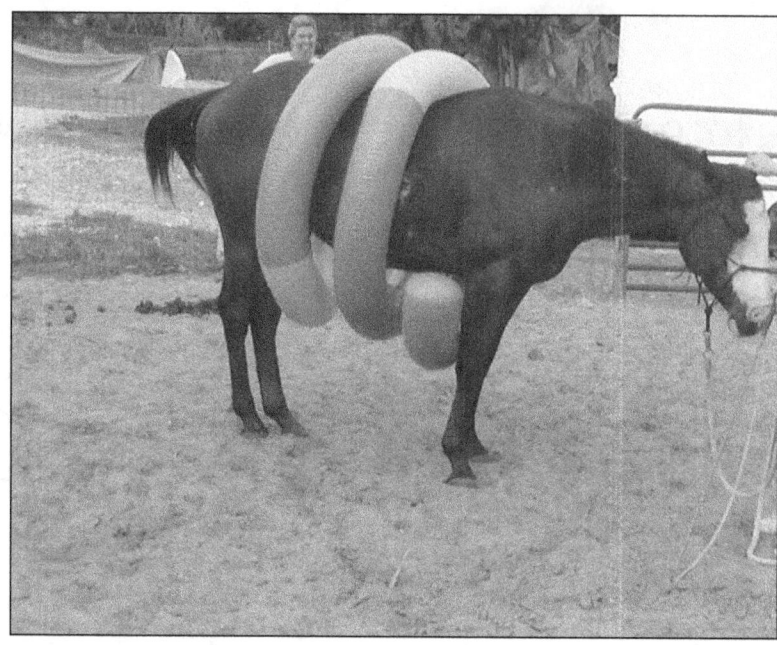

Your horse has a lot to say to you!

We hope these pictures will help you understand how he uses his body to say it. In this picture, Bandit has his feet still, and his head down.

He is <u>accepting</u> of the noodle around his body. Other signs of acceptance are: Ears wiggling, yawning, blinking, or licking his lips. When the horse's head is low, he is relaxed.

In this picture, Cody has both ears forward.

He is showing his attention. There is slack in the rope. He is waiting for what will be asked of him next.

In this picture, Honey's head is level with her withers, and her ears are looking ahead and on her handler.

This shows attentiveness about what is in front of her and what is being asked of her.

Living with Children and Horses

NOTE: This guide is NOT intended as teaching material. It is simply intended to provide a perspective on children and horsemanship based on my own experience.

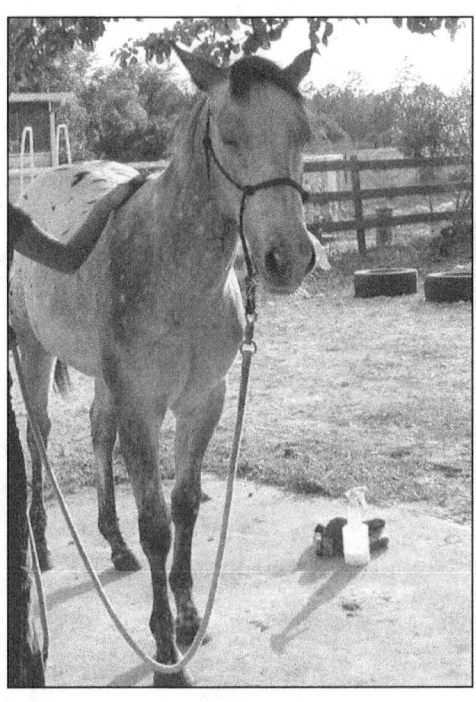

Here Sadie has her eyes closed, and her ears out. She is aware of where her person is, but she is not worried.

Yawning is a good sign that your horse is relaxed.

In this picture, Honey has her head up, and she looks alarmed.
She is showing concern about the obstacles.
If your horse is concerned about something, it is important NOT to add pressure. Give him a few minutes to accept what you are asking.

Living with Children and Horses

NOTE: This guide is NOT intended as teaching material. It is simply intended to provide a perspective on children and horsemanship based on my own experience.

In this picture, Stinker is concerned.

He has his head straight up and his neck is very tight. He is resisting what is asked of him.

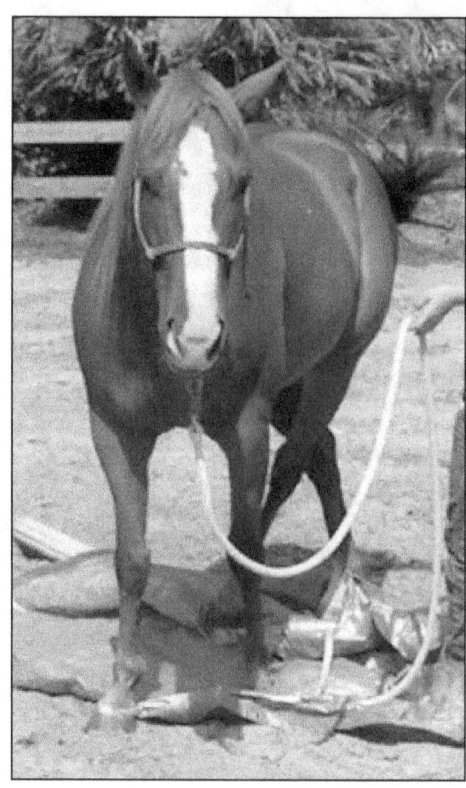

Here, Chunk is happily doing her job.

There is no tension on the rope.

Her eye and his ear are focused on her handler.

In this picture, Majestic is facing her person squarely.

She has her full attention on what is being asked of her.

Living with Children and Horses

In this picture, Sadie is frozen. Her head and neck are stiff and tight and her attention is focused on the gate, and away from her handler.

When a horse looks like this, it is not a good idea to get on it!

In this picture, Teaspoon is thinking about what is asked of her.

One ear is forward, and one ear is back.

She is trying to figure out what the right answer is.

This picture shows another example of a listening horse.

Majestic is focused on doing what is asked of her.

Living with Children and Horses

- 125 -

NOTE: This guide is NOT intended as teaching material. It is simply intended to provide a perspective on children and horsemanship based on my own experience.

Here Buckshot is relaxed.

He is not leaning on the rope.

He has a relaxed walk and a relaxed expression on his face.

In this picture, Buckshot is showing trust and respect for the his handler.

He is standing over a pole, with it between his back legs. Also, his head is bent around toward his handler.

He would not stand quietly like this unless he was relaxed and confident.

Here Bandit is showing signs of concern. He is moving his feet, and his head is raised up. He is also pulling on the rope.

All these things show that he is not comfortable with what he is being asked to do.

In this picture, Bandit is still showing signs of concern. He is leaning on the rope, and the whites of his eyes are showing.

Notice how his right eye is looking away from his person.

His feet will soon follow.

In this picture, Sassy is cooperating, but she is a little close to her handler.

She will need to repeat this exercise slowly until she is more confident at stepping on the tarp.

This picture shows Sassy yawning. Yawning is a sign of relaxation and acceptance.

She is comfortable with her rider standing on the bucket.

She is not worried about being mounted.

Notice the slack in the rope.

Now that you know how to read your horse's body language, you might want to know how to change it! When your horse displays any of the signs of concern, you should SLOW DOWN!

If you are patient and do not demand that he do what you ask when he is worried about it, you can become a better leader for your horse. Slowing down means slowing down. Horses learn when you quit, so you have to be very aware of this. If you quit when he is worried, he will be worse next time. It's your job to read your horse, so you will know BEFORE you push too far and cause him to become upset. This will keep you both safer.

NOTE: This guide is NOT intended as teaching material. It is simply intended to provide a perspective on children and horsemanship based on my own experience.

Here Treasure shows serious signs of concern!

You can see her eyes and ears all looking AWAY from the water.

Living with Children and Horses

NOTE: This guide is NOT intended as teaching material. It is simply intended to provide a perspective on children and horsemanship based on my own experience.

Sometimes it is more important what you DON'T do, than what you do.

Here, I just stayed consistent. Steady hold on the rope. NOT PULLING.

Waiting for her to face me.

When she did face me, she was still thinking about NOT going in the water.

So, I waited. No pressure. Nothing.

After 30 seconds, she got curious about why NOTHING was happening, and took a step forward.

Living with Children and Horses

NOTE: This guide is NOT intended as teaching material. It is simply intended to provide a perspective on children and horsemanship based on my own experience.

I still did NOT PULL her, but held the rope steady and kept waiting.

Another 30 seconds, and

She came forward and got a drink.

Then she got all four feet in the water.

We finished by walking out around the island and back out of the pond.

Living with Children & Horses:
What Horses Give You

NOTE: This guide is NOT intended as teaching material. It is simply intended to provide a perspective on children and horsemanship based on my own experience.

Parents Note: These pictures show how things SHOULD look! Lots of loose ropes, relaxed body language and confident horses who are used to being handled in every area of their bodies. You should not ASSUME that your horses will react the same way. Seek help from a qualified professional if you have issues that are beyond your current skill level. As your awareness rises, your competency will grow. Please visit www.cloud9ranch.info for more references. There are a lot of great books on natural horsemanship and resistance free training.

Remember, every minute you spend with your horse, you ARE teaching him.

It is your responsibility to learn as much as you can, and to keep learning.

Thank you, and Happy Horsing Around!

www.cloud9ranch.info

NOTE: This guide is NOT intended as teaching material. It is simply intended to provide a perspective on children and horsemanship based on my own experience.

What Horses Can Give You

The deer is the Native American symbol of unconditional love. Personally, I think it should be the horse.

When you have a horse of your own… you smile a lot!

Living with Children and Horses

NOTE: This guide is NOT intended as teaching material. It is simply intended to provide a perspective on children and horsemanship based on my own experience.

The best part is that partnership. When they look at you, the same way you look at them. When they whinny when they see you coming! When they run to the gate and say, "PICK ME!"

Living with Children and Horses

NOTE: This guide is NOT intended as teaching material. It is simply intended to provide a perspective on children and horsemanship based on my own experience.

When you can't wait to see your horse, to smell your horse, to be with your horse, you know that this is the way it should be.

Living with Children and Horses — 146 —

NOTE: This guide is NOT intended as teaching material. It is simply intended to provide a perspective on children and horsemanship based on my own experience.

I love it when my horse…

Trusts me enough to NOT worry about the dragons… or alligators!

What can you imagine?

Living with Children and Horses

NOTE: This guide is NOT intended as teaching material. It is simply intended to provide a perspective on children and horsemanship based on my own experience.

Living with Children and Horses   - 149 -

NOTE: This guide is NOT intended as teaching material. It is simply intended to provide a perspective on children and horsemanship based on my own experience.

What Good is Grooming?

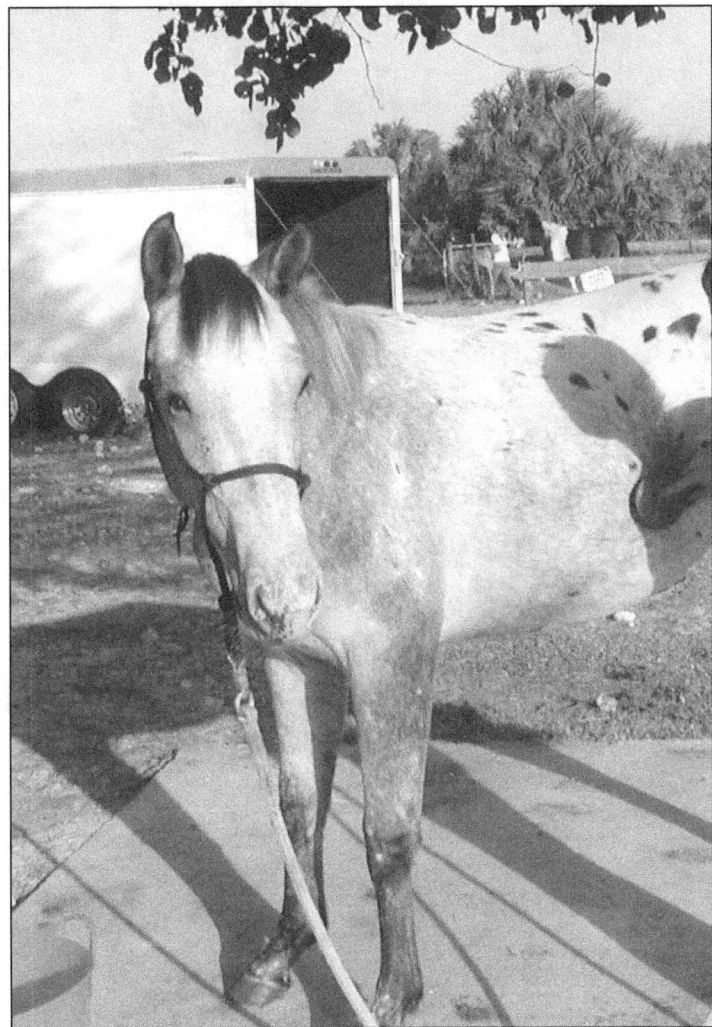

What Good is Grooming?

Before you start to groom your horse, you should gather the things that you will need.

We like to groom using a curry comb, mane and tail brush, three different body brushes (hard, medium and soft), a hoof pick and fly spray.

Be sure to only use the soft brush on the face!

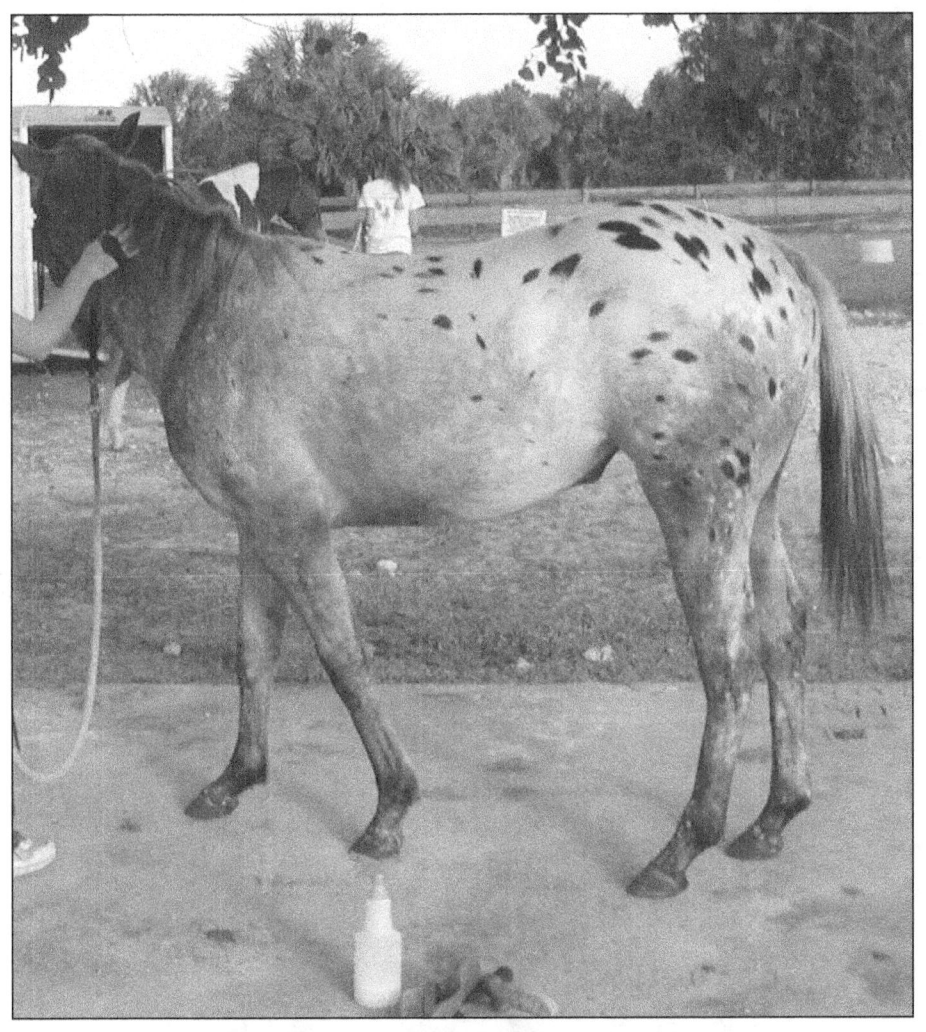

Start by using the curry comb on the neck, chest, legs and body. The curry comb feels good and your horse should like it.
It's nice when your horse can stand with you, on a loose line, and not be tied up. If you can't do this at first, have someone help you by holding the rope.

After a few sessions, your horse should stand quietly with you
while you groom her.

Living with Children and Horses

NOTE: This guide is NOT intended as teaching material. It is simply intended to provide a perspective on children and horsemanship based on my own experience.

Be sure that you spend the same amount of time
on both sides of the horse.

Curry comb first, then brushes. Some horses like hard brushes, and some prefer softer brushes.
The curry comb picks up the dirt and hair, and the next brush brushes it off. Your horse should feel clean and soft after brushing.

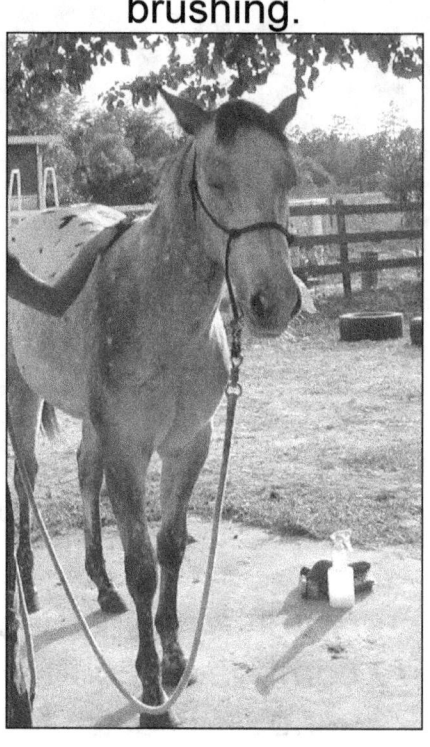

A good grooming is like a massage.
It should be relaxing for you and for your horse.

When you find your horse's favorite spots, she may let you know you found it by raising up her lip,
or holding her neck out in a funny way.

Ooooo, that's a good spot!

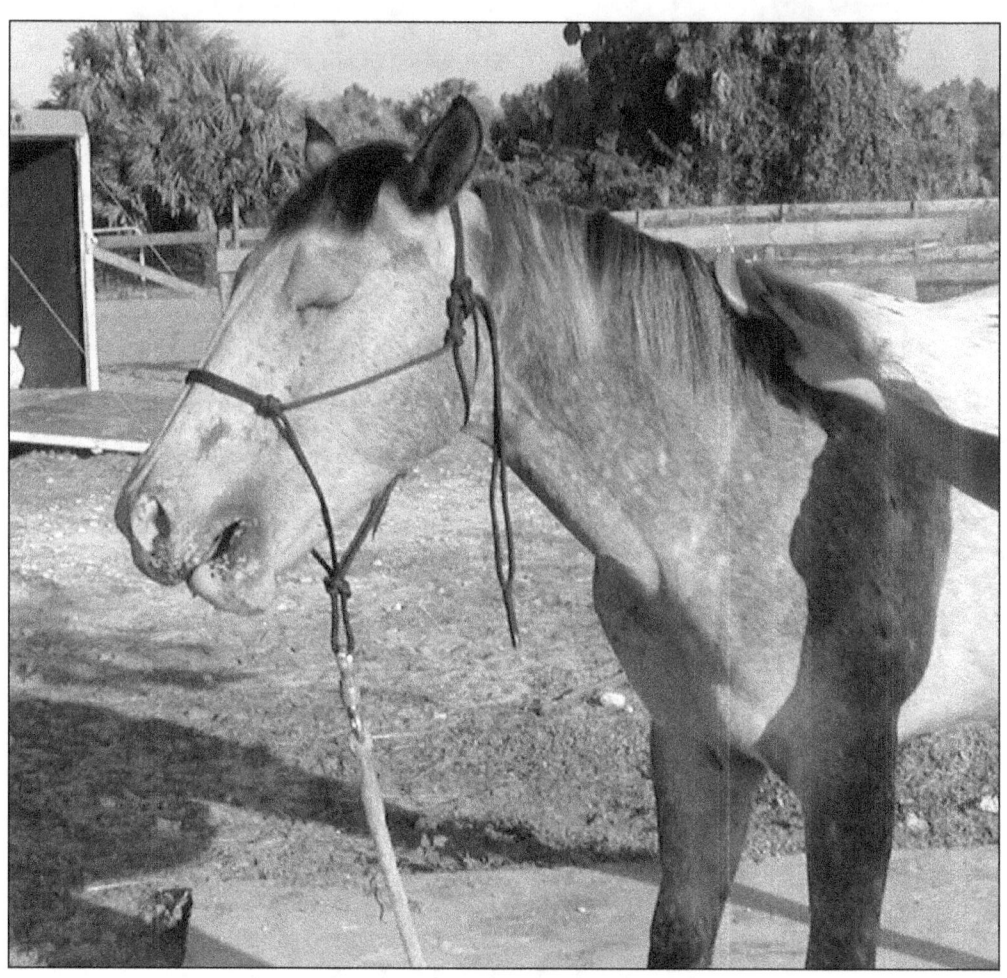

Yawning is a good sign
that your horse is relaxed.

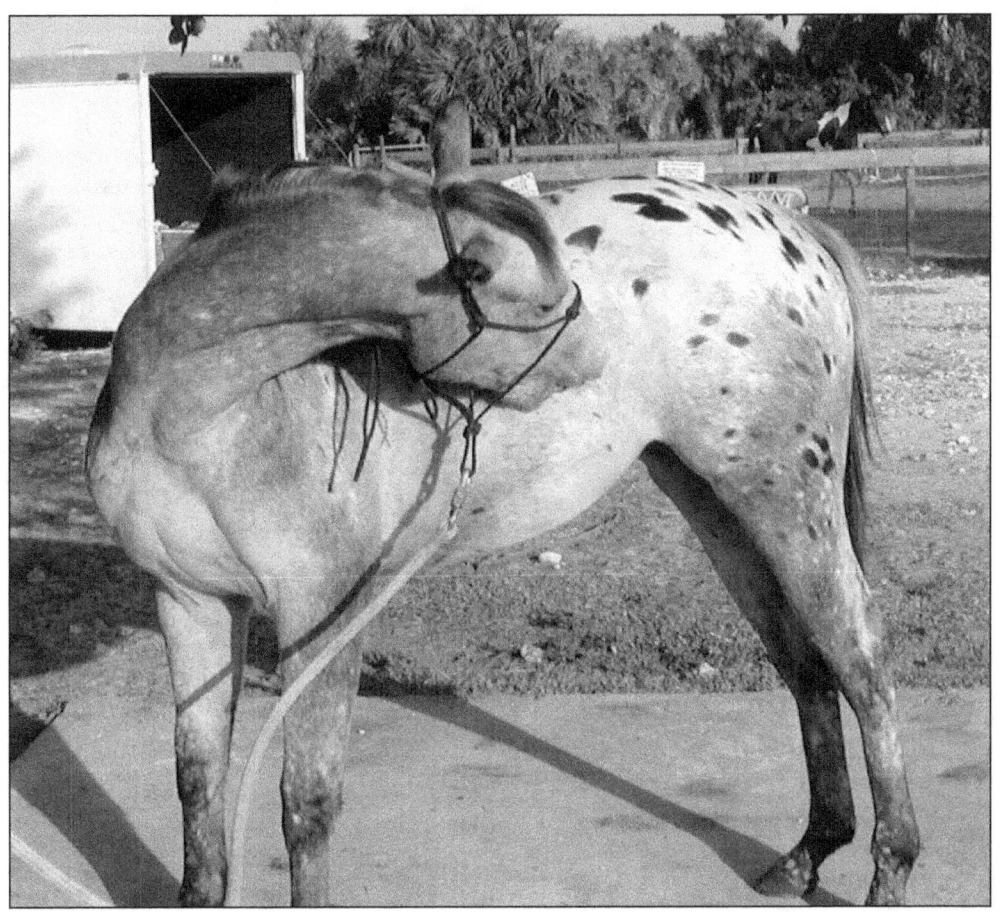

Pay attention to what your horse is telling you.

Here, Sadie is asking for a scratch right there.

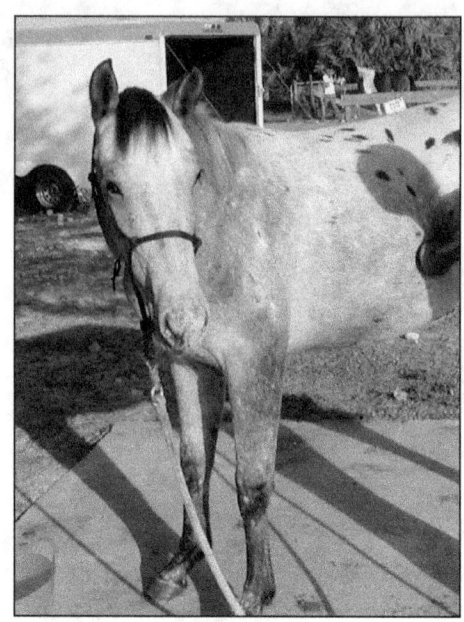

When you help her get her itchy spots,
she will look forward to having you groom her.

It's an important part of developing your relationship.

That's the right spot!

Keep scratching!

Living with Children and Horses

NOTE: This guide is NOT intended as teaching material. It is simply intended to provide a perspective on children and horsemanship based on my own experience.

When you brush your horse's tail, be sure to stand off to the side.

Hold the rope so that you can use it to turn your horse to face you if you need to.

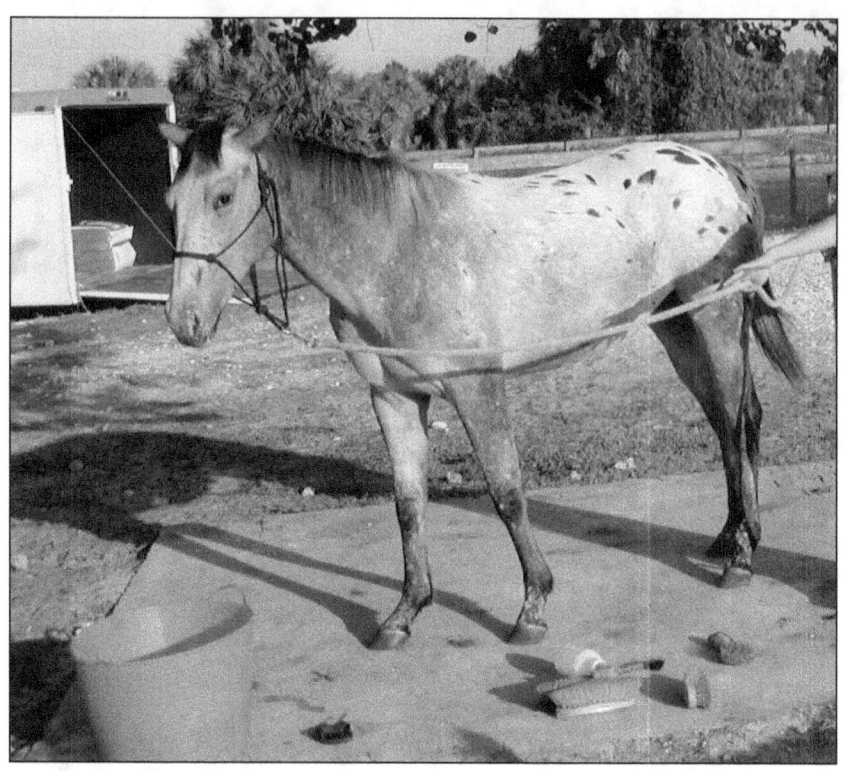

Shorten the rope until you can bring her nose toward your belly button.

Without moving <u>your</u> feet, you can safely have the horse turn and face you.

Don't forget to brush your horse's face and ears.

Use the softest brush you have for this job.

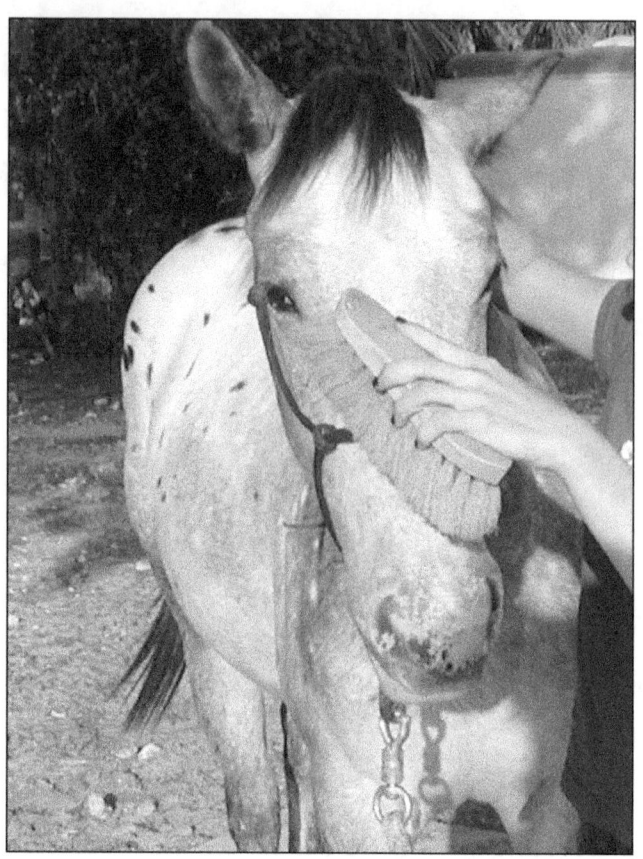

If your horse says "NO! I am afraid to have you brush my face!" (Or pick up my feet, or brush my tail!) then you should ask for help from someone who has more experience than you do.

Don't ever try to <u>make</u> a horse do something they are uncomfortable doing. This can be dangerous.
If you are patient, and ask the horse to <u>try</u> to cooperate with you, you will be surprised how easily you can change her mind.

NOTE: This guide is NOT intended as teaching material. It is simply intended to provide a perspective on children and horsemanship based on my own experience.

I am the LEADER!

I like playing with my horse, Maude. She waits patiently for me all day, while I do my chores and schoolwork. When it is time to play, I try to make it enjoyable for both of us.

It is fun to play horse games.
She thinks she may play better than I do... but
I convince her to follow me.

I am the leader,
so when I back up, she backs up with me.

I want her to enjoy being near me. But if she wants to leave, I help her go.

Living with Children and Horses

NOTE: This guide is NOT intended as teaching material. It is simply intended to provide a perspective on children and horsemanship based on my own experience.

After I move her feet and control her direction, she asks if she can come back to me.

Now, she understands that I am the leader.

Living with Children and Horses

NOTE: This guide is NOT intended as teaching material. It is simply intended to provide a perspective on children and horsemanship based on my own experience.

If she forgets to pay attention to me, I move her hindquarters until her attention comes back.

I like being the leader.

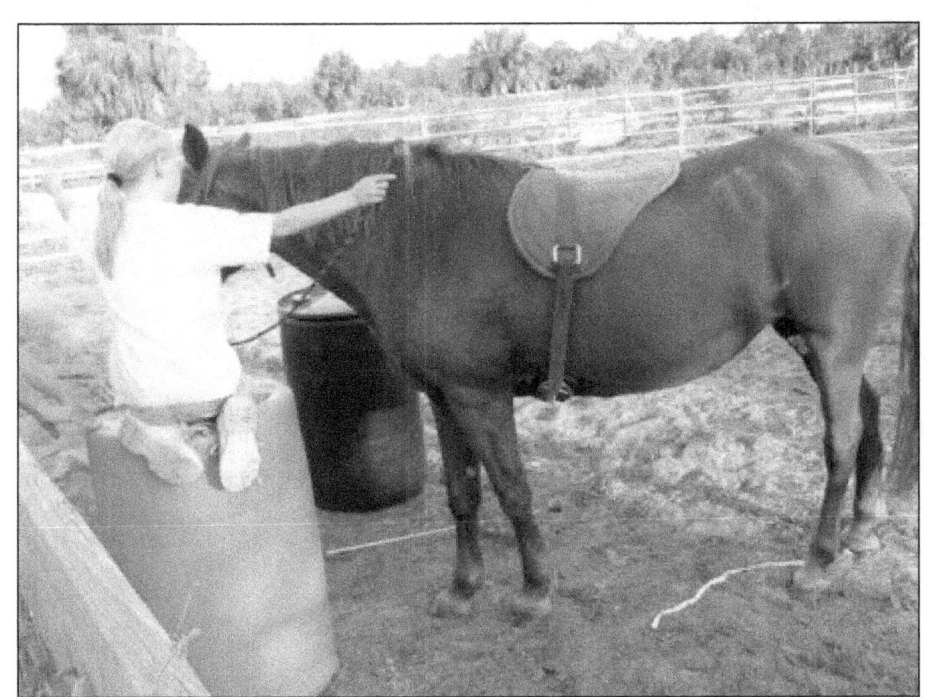

When we are ready, I ask my horse to pick me up.

Living with Children and Horses

NOTE: This guide is NOT intended as teaching material. It is simply intended to provide a perspective on children and horsemanship based on my own experience.

She stands quietly while I get on.

My horse will do whatever
I ask of her.

That's because I am
a good leader.

Body Language Defined:

You can tell a lot by the look on someone's face....

Take a look at what the body language in these pictures is saying:

Defensive:

Head Up
Ears Back
Eyes Looking Away
Legs Braced
Lips and Tail Tight

Living with Children and Horses

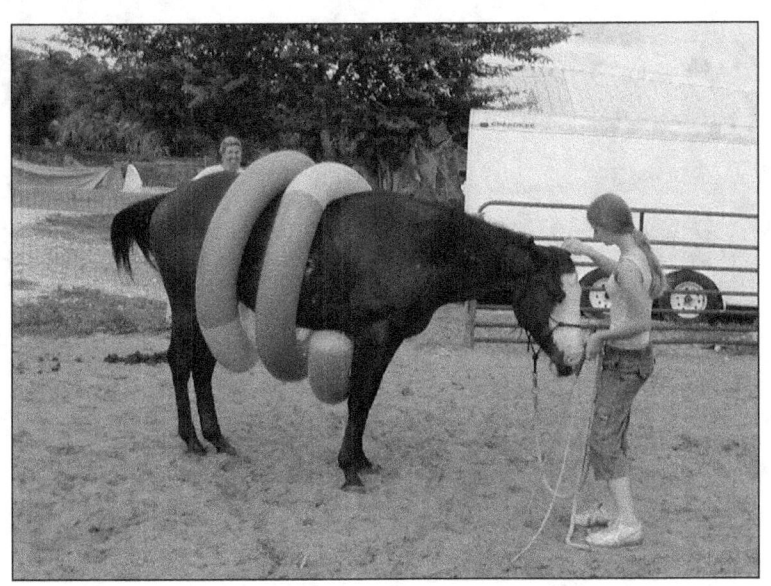

Accepting

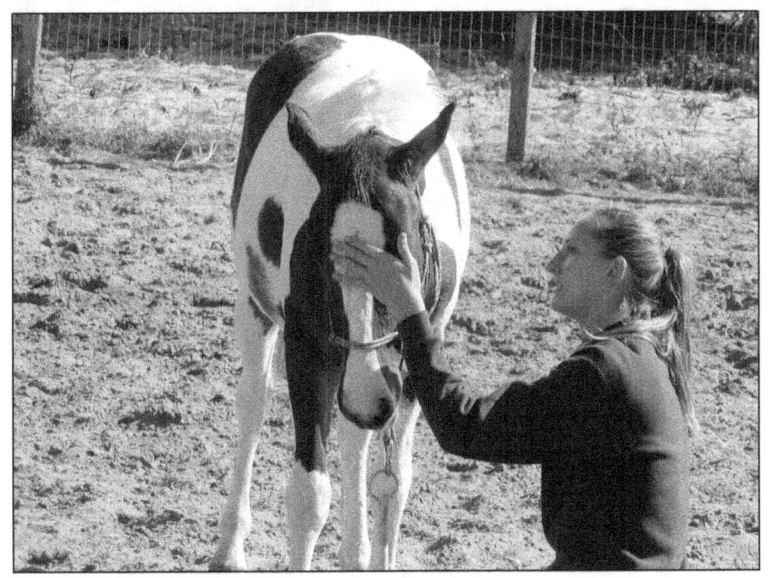

Head Down
Ears Relaxed
Eyes Soft
Licking Lips

Living with Children and Horses

NOTE: This guide is NOT intended as teaching material. It is simply intended to provide a perspective on children and horsemanship based on my own experience.

ATTENTIVE:

Eyes and Ear on Handler
Ears Relaxed
Eyes Soft
Licking Lips

Living with Children and Horses — 173 —

NOTE: This guide is NOT intended as teaching material. It is simply intended to provide a perspective on children and horsemanship based on my own experience.

Cooperative:

Eye and Ear on Handler
Ears Relaxed
Eyes Soft
Licking Lips
Float in rope, not pulling, not slack

Concerned:

Eye and Ear looking for escape
Tight Mouth and Lips
Heavy on Rope, Going Backwards

Relaxed:

Head Down
Accepting of touch on face, head, ears
Licking Lips
Yawning
Relaxed tail and lips

Living with Children and Horses

NOTE: This guide is NOT intended as teaching material. It is simply intended to provide a perspective on children and horsemanship based on my own experience.

Relaxed:

Head down
Ears relaxed
Eyes soft
Licking lips and yawning

Concerned:

Head up
Whites of Eyes showing
Leaning on Rope
Moving feet too quickly or not at all
Tail tight

Cooperating, but unsure:

Doing what is asked, BUT
Head is up
Ears are back
Too close to handler
Need more time to investigate object (tarp)

Living with Children and Horses

Cooperative:

Eye and ear on handler
Ears relaxed
Eyes soft
Licking lips
Float in rope, not pulling, not slack

Living with Children and Horses

NOTE: This guide is NOT intended as teaching material. It is simply intended to provide a perspective on children and horsemanship based on my own experience.

Curious:

Head neutral
Ears relaxed
Eyes soft
Licking lips

Living with Children and Horses

NOTE: This guide is NOT intended as teaching material. It is simply intended to provide a perspective on children and horsemanship based on my own experience.

The Riding Lesson

Living with Children and Horses

- 182 -

NOTE: This guide is NOT intended as teaching material. It is simply intended to provide a perspective on children and horsemanship based on my own experience.

A riding lesson is a good time to ask questions. Here, Mojo is not very comfortable about Amanda waving the stick around.

Her instructor is offering support and advice. We use calm repetition to reassure the horse that we are not a threat.
That means, you repeat the action in a casual manner until the horse accepts it.

Next, Amanda checks to see how responsive her horse is to moving away from her fingers.

When she is riding, she will need the horse to move away from her legs and reins when she asks.

As the session continues, Mojo gets more relaxed and confident with her small handler.

When she is calm and cooperative, Amanda may ask her to pick her up, so she can ride.

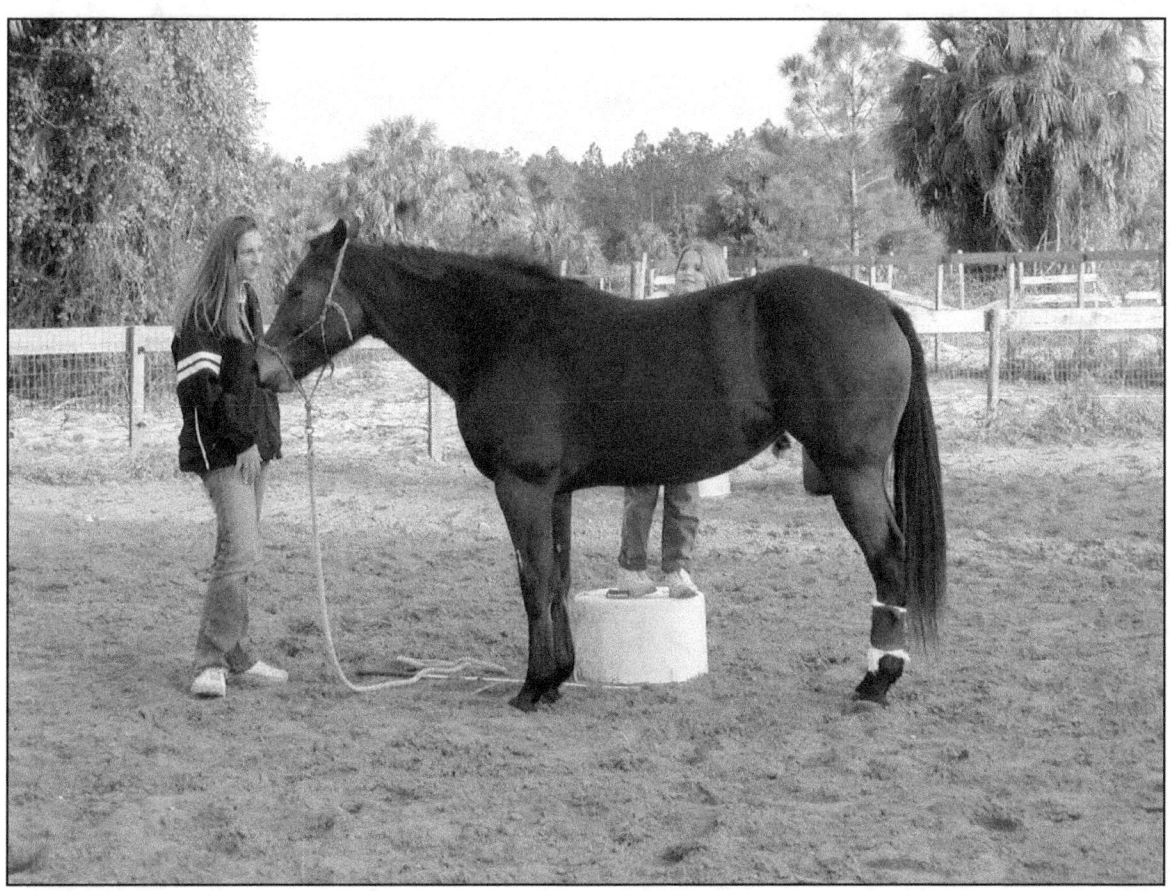

Here the instructor is close by in case she is needed, but Amanda gets to learn how to ask the horse to step into position on her own.

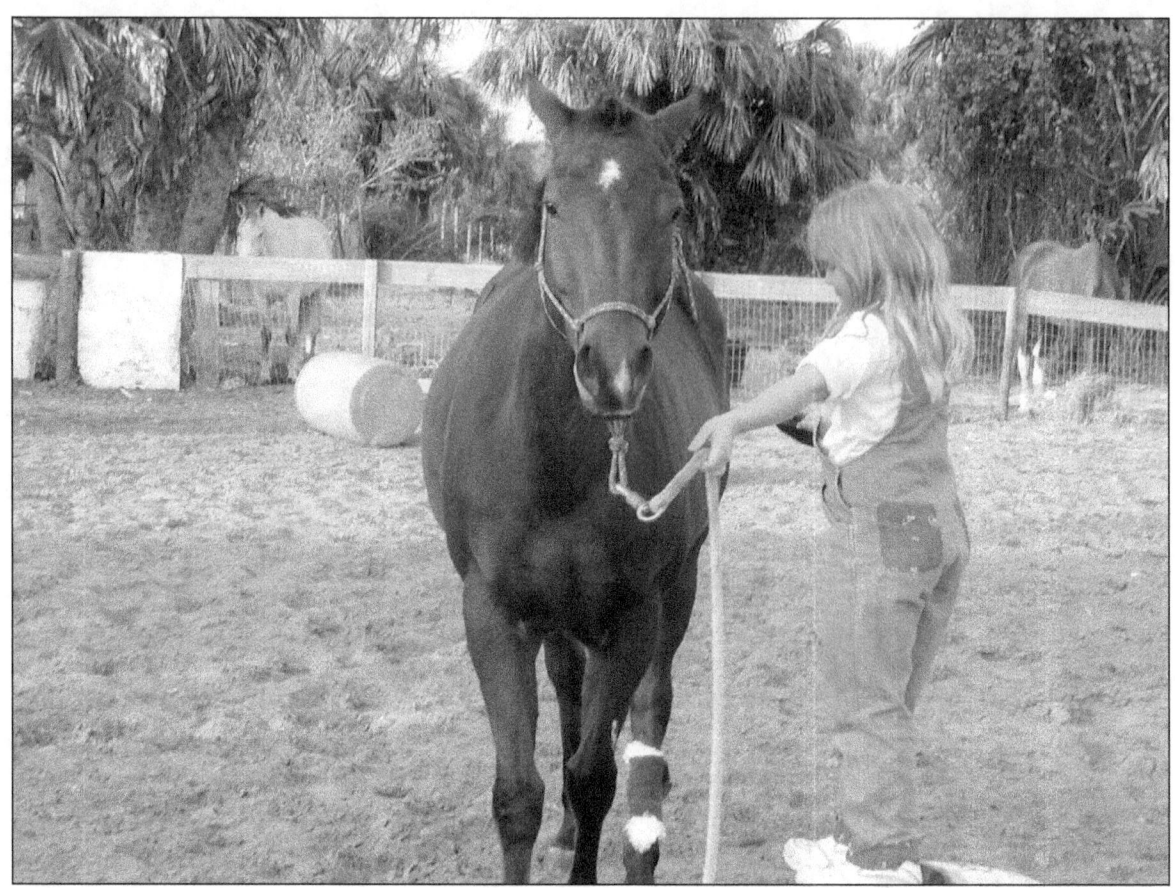

Amanda asks her to step up one step.

Then she can mount.

When Amanda is mounted, the instructor can move her horse around and let Amanda find her balance. It is important that each rider be allowed to find their balance BEFORE they have to worry about directing the horse.

Are You Ready to Ride?

Living with Children and Horses — 189 —

NOTE: This guide is NOT intended as teaching material. It is simply intended to provide a perspective on children and horsemanship based on my own experience.

If your horse comes to you happily, without you having to <u>catch</u> him,
you may be ready to ride!

When you ask your horse to do something, like go between the barrels or jump a small obstacle, and he is glad to do it, you may be ready to ride!

Living with Children and Horses

NOTE: This guide is NOT intended as teaching material. It is simply intended to provide a perspective on children and horsemanship based on my own experience.

If you can not control your horses' feet when you are standing next to him, then your chances are not much better when you get on!

In fact, your chances are less. Don't get on your horse until things are working well on the ground. This will help keep you safe!

Living with Children and Horses

NOTE: This guide is NOT intended as teaching material. It is simply intended to provide a perspective on children and horsemanship based on my own experience.

A horse that is happy and comfortable with his rider is fun to ride, and he will enjoy it as much as you do!

When it is time to ride, ask your horse to pick you up.

If he won't stand still next to something for you to get on,

he is telling you he is not ready for you to ride.

Once you are on your horse, try to use as little pressure as necessary to communicate what you want him to do.

Remember, a horse is sensitive! He can feel a fly land on his hair, so he can definitely feel your leg muscles tighten and relax on his sides.

When you have communication, there is no need for force.

When you are riding, see if your horse can follow your focus.
When you turn your shoulders and hips, he should turn his body also.

The most important part of riding is developing good balance.

When you are beginning to learn to ride, it is a good idea to get the balance part down first, by having someone lead you around, before you worry about trying to steer the horse.

A good rider is developed over time, and earns the right to ride. Don't rush your basics!

www.ingramcontent.com/pod-product-compliance
Lightning Source LLC
Chambersburg PA
CBHW081154290426
44108CB00018B/2543